Local Public Schools

Public Policy
Bibliographies: 2

Local Public Schools: How to Pay for Them?

Compiled by

DOROTHY CAMPBELL TOMPKINS

INSTITUTE OF GOVERNMENTAL STUDIES
University of California, Berkeley, 1972

Library of Congress Cataloging in Publication Data:

Tompkins, Dorothy Louise (Campbell) Culver.
  Local public schools: How to pay for them?

  (Public policy bibliographies, 2)
  1. Education—California—Finance—Bibliography.
  I. Title. II. Series.
  Z5814.F5T65   016.3791'09794   72–4083

International Standard Book Number: 0-87772-152-1

$3.50

PREFACE

The California Supreme Court decision last August, concerning
public school financing, prompted the compilation of this bibliography. It covers materials in public administration, law,
education, and state and local government since 1965. It is
concerned with how to provide school money rather than how to
spend it.

In the preparation of this bibliography, use has been made of
the Libraries of the University of California, Berkeley, particularly the Education-Psychology, Graduate Social Science,
Law School, and Institute of Governmental Studies Libraries.

To the many officials throughout the country who have provided
me with materials, I make grateful acknowledgment. To my col-
leagues in the Institute of Governmental Studies for their assistance, to Judy Rasmussen for her part in preparing the manuscript for publication, and to John Barr Tompkins for his reading of the manuscript, I express my gratitude.

Dorothy C. Tompkins

July 1972

CONTENTS

	Page
Inequality of Educational Opportunity........................	1
Financing of Local Public Schools........................	14
State Financing of Local Public Schools.................	24
Federal Assistance in Financing Local Public Schools...	60
Programs and Proposals for Financing Local Public	
Schools..	68
Performance Contracting............................	68
Voucher System.....................................	75
Value-added Tax....................................	81
Index...	90

INEQUALITY OF EDUCATIONAL OPPORTUNITY

"The distinctive and priceless function of education in our society, warrants, indeed compels, our treating it as a fundamental interest.... Education is essential in maintaining what several commentators have termed free enterprise democracy--that is, preserving an individual's opportunity to compete successfully in the economic marketplace, despite a disadvantaged background.... Education is universally relevant... public education continues over a lengthy period of life--between 10 and 13 years. Few other government services have such sustained, intensive contact with the recipient.... Education is unmatched in the extent to which it molds the personality of the youth of society.... Education is so important that the state has made it compulsory."

California. Supreme Court
Serrano v. Priest, no. L.A. 29820. 5 C. 3d 584
(August 30, 1971)   1

California school financing scheme flunks equal
protection clause test. United States Law Week
40: 1033-34, 2128-29, September 14, 1971   2

On August 30, 1971, the California Supreme Court found that "the California public school financing system with its substantial dependence on local property taxes and resultant wide disparities in school revenue, violates the equal protection clause of the Fourteenth Amendment.... Recognizing as we must that the right to an education in our public schools is a fundamental interest which cannot be conditioned on wealth, we can discern no compelling state purpose necessitating the present methods of financing.... Such a system cannot withstand constitutional challenge and must fall before the equal protection clause."

The Court modified its Serrano opinion on October 21, 1971, by pointing out that it did not constitute a final judgment on the merits and that the existing system of school finance is to remain in effect until it has been found unconstitutional and replaced by an appropriate new system (United States Law Week 40: 2339, December 7, 1971).

California school tax system may continue.
National Civic Review 60: 632, December
1971   *3

* Available in the Library of the Institute of Governmental Studies, University of California, Berkeley.

1

Materials relating to Serrano v. Priest include the following:

Abelson, Stuart
  Property taxes for school finance. Inequality in Education
  (Harvard Center for Law and Education) (10): 10-11, Decem-
  ber 1971   4

Adams, John K.
  The California decision--and what was behind it. Georgia
  County Government Magazine, March 1972: 54-58+   5

  California school tax ruling; what does it mean? Opportunity (U.S. Office of Economic Opportunity), January-February
  1972: 2-7   6

Bateman, Worth and Brown, Peter
  Some reflections on Serrano v. Priest. Journal of Urban
  Law 49: 701-10, May 1972   7

Boynton, Ralph E.
  The economics of school finance. Pacific Business (California Chamber of Commerce) 61: 39, November-December 1971   *8

Brown, Robert C.
  The meaning of Serrano versus Priest; before Associated Taxpayers of Idaho, December 1971.
  Reprinted: New York State Taxpayer 3: 7, January-February
  1972   *9

California. Judicial Council. Administrative Office of the
  Courts
  California school financing system held unconstitutional by
  Supreme Court [Serrano v. Priest]. 64p (mim) (News re-
  lease #111) San Francisco, August 30, 1971   *10

California. Legislature. Senate. Committee on Education and
  Select Committee on School District Finance
  Serrano v. Priest--implications for school finance; proceedings of hearing, Sacramento, October 20, 1971. 132p+ (process) Sacramento, 1971   *11

California. Supreme Court
  John Serrano, Jr. v. Ivy Baker Priest, Los Angeles no.
  29,820; amici curiae brief of the Urban Coalition, National
  Committee for the Support of the Public Schools; by John E.
  Coons and Stephen D. Sugarman. 44p January 4, 1971   *12

California court case strikes down property taxes for schools.
  Urban Information Newsletter (International City Management
  Association), January-February 1972: 2-3

California's public school financing system held to violate
equal protection clause. Tax Administrators News (Federation of Tax Administrators) 35: 97-98, September 1971   *14

Cassidy, Joseph
Property tax decision (California). Compact (Education Commission of the States) 5: 38-39, December 1971   *15

Catholic University. School of Law. Center for National Policy
Review
Educational finance formulas and the Serrano decision. Its
Clearinghouse for Civil Rights Research 1 (1): 4-5, March
1972   *16

Coons, John E.
The case for equal tax support for the state's schools. San
Francisco Sunday Examiner and Chronicle, This World, Novem-
ber 14, 1971: 22   17

Equal dollars for school districts. New York Times, November 1, 1971: 41   18

Court looks hard at school taxes; editorial. Pacific Business
Bulletin (California Chamber of Commerce) 61: 8, November 1,
1971   *19

Curran, William J.
Social change and health law: the court as can-opener; the
legislature as soup. American Journal of Public Health 61:
2518-19, December 1971   *20

Dividing the cake. Time Magazine, September 13, 1971: 47   21

Doyle, Denis P.
Court decision shakes school tax structure. California Journal 2: 237+, September 1971   *22

Education Commission of the States
Serrano v. Priest; [summary of legislative seminar, Houston,
December 1, 1971]. 12p (mim) Denver, 1971   *23
        Presentations by Stephen Sugarman and
        John Silard.

Flournoy, Houston I.
Serrano and the future of school finance. State Government
45: 78-82, Spring 1972   *24

Goldstein, Stephen R.
Interdistrict inequalities in school financing; a critical
analysis of Serrano v. Priest and its progeny. University
of Pennsylvania Law Review 120: 504-44, January 1972   25

Grieder, Calvin
  California tax case raises tough questions. Nation's
  Schools 88: 14, December 1971   26

Hamilton, Lee
  The future of the local school property tax. NAM Reports
  (National Association of Manufacturers) 16: 8-11, November
  15, 1971   *27

Hickey, John K.
  Serrano--quo vadis? State Government 45: 83-88, Spring 1972
                                                             *28

International Association of Assessing Officers
  Repercussions of California tax ruling; by Philip E. Watson
  and Harold Webb, before third general session, September 22,
  1971. IAAO Newsletter 37: 186-87, November 1971   *29

Karst, Kenneth L.
  Serrano v. Priest: a state court's responsibilities and opportunities in the development of federal constitutional
  law. California Law Review 60: 720-56, May 1972   *30

Keiter, Robert B.
  California educational financing system violates equal protection. Clearinghouse Review (National Clearinghouse for
  Legal Services, Northwestern University Law School) 5: 287-
  88, October 1971   *31

Lawyers' Committee for Civil Rights Under Law
  School taxing and spending systems valid under Serrano v.
  Priest; by John E. Coons. 8p (mim) Washington, D.C.,
  December 1971   *32
  Excerpt: Compact (Education Commission of the States) 6: 39-
  41, April 1972

Myers, Phyllis
  Second thoughts on the Serrano case. City 5: 38-41, Winter
  1971   *33
  Same: Principles of the American dream. Sunday Star, Janu-
  ary 9, 1972
  Reprinted: Congressional Record, January 18, 1972: E8-10
  Excerpt: Compact (Education Commission of the States) 6: 42-
  45, April 1972

New financing for schools; editorial. America 125: 363,
  November 6, 1971   34

New York State Conference of Mayors and Other Municipal Officials
California school decision. Its Legal Bulletin, October
1971: 4119-20   *35

Reinhold, Robert
John Serrano Jr. et al., and school tax equality. New York
Times, January 10, 1972: 1E   36
Reprinted: Congressional Record, February 3, 1972: S1127-32

Resnick, Michael A.
Serrano v. Priest: blueprint for tax reform? Nation's
Schools 89: 43-45, March 1972   37

A school-tax ruling that could overturn financing in most
states. U.S. News and World Report, September 13, 1971: 90
                                                                *38

Serrano v. Priest: implications for educational equality,
with commentary of William N. Greenbaum. Harvard Educational Review 41: 501-34, November 1971   39

Serrano v. Priest; [California] State Supreme Court shakes up
school finance; nationwide effect. Cal-Tax News (California
Taxpayers' Association) 12: 1, October 1971   *40

U.S. Advisory Commission on Intergovernmental Relations
School finance court decision [text of Serrano v. Priest].
64p (process) Washington, D.C., September 15, 1971   *41

A welcome blow at the school tax; editorial. Fortune 79: 68,
October 1971   42

Who pays for tomorrow's schools: the emerging issues of school
finance equalization. Yale Review of Law and Social Action
2: 108-67, Winter 1971   43
               A first appraisal of Serrano, by John E.
               Coons and others;
               School finance equalization lawsuits: a
               model legislative response, by Arthur E.
               Wise;
               Serrano--a victory of sorts for ethics,
               not necessarily for education, by Paul
               R. Dimond;
               Serrano in the political arena, by David
               L. Kirp and Mark G. Yudof.

Wise, Arthur E.
Financing schools: property tax is obsolete; the California
doctrine. Saturday Review, November 20, 1971: 78-79+   44

Zukosky, Jerome
   Education, housing reform offer new regional prospect.
   National Civic Review 61: 128-35, March 1972   *45

Serrano was not the first challenge to state educational financing systems. Disparities in educational expenditures had
been before the courts in Illinois (McGinnis v. Shapiro, 293 F.
Supp. 327 (1968), 394 U.S. 322 (1969)), in Virginia (Burrus v.
Wilkerson, 310 F. Supp. 572 (1969), 397 U.S. 44 (1970)), and
in Florida (Hargrave v. Kirk, 313 F. Supp. 944 (1970)).

      Keiter, Robert R.
      California educational financing system vio-
      lates equal protection. Clearinghouse Review
      (National Clearinghouse for Legal Services,
      Northwestern University) 5: 287-88, October
      1971   *46

Serrano has been followed quickly by a series of similar legal
actions in several states to eliminate the general reliance of
school financing on local property taxes--Texas, Minnesota and
New Jersey.

      Legal "box score" on school financing issue.
      Education Commission of the States, Bulletin
      4: 2, February 1972   *47

Materials relating to these and other legal actions concerning
school financing include the following:

Andrews, Frederick
   Tax-revolution: court-backed effort to equalize schooling
   promises an upheaval. Wall Street Journal, March 2, 1972:1+
                                                            48

A bad way to pay for schools [in California and New Jersey].
   Life Magazine, December 10, 1971: 42   49

Cohen, David K.
   The economics of inequality [concerning MacInnes v. Ogil-
   vie before U.S. Supreme Court, March 25, 1969]. Saturday
   Review, April 19, 1969: 64-65+   50

Courts find California, Minnesota, Texas school financing systems unconstitutional. State Government News (Council of
   State Governments) 15: 2-3, January 1972   *51

Education Commission of the States
Understanding education's financial dilemma; the impact of
Serrano-type court decisions on American education; by Clifford L. Dochterman and others. 41p (School finance series
no. 1) Denver, April 1972   *52

Federation of Tax Administrators
School finance, the property tax and the courts. 25p (RM-425) Chicago, March 1972   53

Kolesar, John
Prospects improve for court challenge to local school property tax system. Public Issues (Center for Analysis of Public Issues, Princeton, N.J.) 1 (6): 2-3, November 1971   *54

Landmark court decisions herald change for assessors [in California and Texas]. IAAO Newsletter (International Association of Assessing Officials) 38: 19, February 1972   *55

New Jersey and Texas add to Serrano suits. Cal-Tax News (California Taxpayers' Association) 13: 3, March 1972   *56

New Jersey. Superior Court, Hudson County
[Robinson v. Cahill, January 19, 1972.]   *57
Comment: New Jersey school funding voided. State Government
News (Council of State Governments) 15: 4, February 1972
Comment: New Jersey court voids school finance. National
Civic Review 61: 147-48, March 1972

New York State. Supreme Court. Westchester County
Spano v. Board of Education of Lakeland Central School, District #1, Yorktown and others; decision of Joseph F. Hawkins. 10p (Index no. 10510, 1971) White Plains, January
17, 1972   *58
Comment: Court upholds state on school financing, by M.A.
Farber. New York Times, January 19, 1972: 33
Comment: New York Court dismisses a Serrano suit. Cal-Tax
News (California Taxpayers' Association) 13: 3, March 1972

School finance cases filed and in process. U.S. Senate Select Committee on Equal Educational Opportunity, Equal educational opportunity--1971; hearings pt. 16D-2, p. 8275-77   *59

School financing upheld in New York, ruled invalid in New Jersey, Arizona [Hollins v. Shofstall, January 13, 1972]. Tax
Administrators News (Federation of Tax Administrators) 36:
21, February 1972   *60

Tax Reform Research Group
  Reforms listed for federal, state, and local levels. Its
  Property Tax Newsletter, November 1971   61
      Recent court decisions have "held that a
      state cannot set any system of paying for
      public educations that makes the amount of
      money available in any particular district
      or for any particular child, dependent up-
      on local wealth."
  Reprinted: Congressional Record, March 16, 1972: E2669-72

U.S. Advisory Commission on Intergovernmental Relations
  School finance; new challenge to federalism. 13p (process)
  (Bulletin no. 72-1) Washington, D.C., March 8, 1972   *62

U.S. District Court. District of Minnesota, Third Division
  Van Dusartz v. Hatfield; memorandum and order (No. 3-71
  Civ. 243). October 12, 1971   *63
  Reprinted: Congressional Record, January 18, 1972: E6-8
  Comment: Van Dusartz v. Hatfield. Tax Administrators News
  (Federation of Tax Administrators) 36: 8, January 1972

U.S. District Court. Western District of Texas, San Antonio
  Division
  Rodriguez v. San Antonio Independent School District (No.
  63-175-SA Civ.). December 23, 1971   64
  Reprinted: Congressional Record, January 18, 1972: E4-6
  Comment: U.S. Court upset Texas school tax tied to property.
  New York Times, December 25, 1971: 1+
  Comment: Texas decision spurs public school financing con-
  troversy. Rhode Island University, Bureau of Government Re-
  search, Newsletter 13: 1, January 1972
  Comment: A fresh blow against financing schools with prop-
  erty taxes. U.S. News and World Report, January 10, 1972:
  66
  Comment: Federal court voids Texas tax. National Civic Re-
  view 61: 91, February 1972
  Comment: Court clears Texas school bonds for two years.
  MFOA Newsletter (Municipal Finance Offices Association of
  the United States and Canada) 47: 16, February 16, 1972

Walker, Mabel
  Fiscal problems of fractionated governments; with special
  reference to property taxation. Tax Policy (Tax Institute
  of America) 38 (10-12), October-December 1971   *65
      Decisions relating to educational and tax
      disparities in financing education, p. 16-17.

Westmeyer, Troy R. and Wesley, eds.
  School finance suits intensify: federal funding urged to
  equalize opportunity. National Civic Review 60: 576-77,
  November 1971   *66

Wisconsin. Legislative Council
  The public school financing cases: Serrano, Van Dusartz,
  Rodriguez, Sweetwater County and Robinson. 17p (Staff
  brief 72-5) Madison, January 21, 1972, revised May 1,
  1972   *67

Materials relating to inequality of educational opportunity
include the following:

Campbell, Alan K.
  Inequities of school finance. Saturday Review, January 11,
  1969: 44+   68

Carter, Robert L.
  Equal educational opportunity--an overview. Black Law Journal 1: 197-205, Winter 1971   69

Chicago. University. Center for Policy Study
  The quality of inequality: urban and suburban public schools;
  report of a conference; edited by Charles U. Daly. 160p
  Chicago, 1968   70
          The constitution and equal educational
          opportunity, by Arthur E. Wise;
          Equal educational opportunity, or the
          limits of constitutional jurisprudence
          undefined, by Philip B. Kurland;
          Quality and inequality: some economic
          issues related to the choice of educa-
          tional policy, by Otto A. Davis.
  Excerpt: Equal educational opportunity, by Philip B. Kur-
  land. University of Chicago Law Review 35: 583-600, 1968

Committee for Economic Development
  The conditions for educational equality; edited by Sterling
  M. McMurrin. 203p (Supplementary paper no. 34) New York,
  July 1971   *71
          The meanings of equality, by James L.
          Jarrett;
          Increasing educational opportunity, by
          James S. Coleman.

Developments in the law--equal protection. Harvard Law Review
  82: 1065-192, March 1969   72
          New standards of equality--education,
          p. 183-89.

Discriminations against the poor and the Fourteenth Amendment.
Harvard Law Review 81: 435-53, December 1967   73
Education, p. 452-53.

Equal educational opportunity; symposium. Harvard Educational
Review 38: 3-175, Winter 1968   74
The constitutional dimensions of equal
educational opportunity, by David Kirp;
School factors and equal educational op-
portunity, by Henry S. Dyer;
The concept of equality of educational
opportunity, by James S. Coleman.

Graham, Robert L. and Kravitt, Jason H.
The evolution of equal protection--education, municipal
services and wealth. Harvard Civil Rights-Civil Liberties
Law Review 7: 103-213, January 1972   *75
Appendix: Law suits challenging state
school finance systems.

Guthrie, James W.
The roots of educational inequality and suggestions for reform. In U.S. Senate Select Committee on Equal Educational
Opportunity, Equal educational opportunity, hearings, September 1970, pt. 7, p. 3401-11   *76

Guthrie, James W. and Others
Dollars for schools: the reinforcement of inequality. Educational Administration Quarterly 6: 32-45, Autumn 1970   77

Harvard Center for Law and Education
School financing and the Fourteenth Amendment; by James A.
Bensfield. 19p (Inequality in education no. 1) Cambridge,
1969   78

Hickrod, G. Alan and Sabulao, Cesar M.
Increasing social and economic inequalities among suburban
schools: a study in educational administration and finance.
v.p. Danville, Ill., Interstate Printers and Publishers,
Inc., 1969   79

Horowitz, Harold W.
Unseparate but unequal--the emerging Fourteenth Amendment
issue in public school education. UCLA Law Review 13: 1147-
72, August 1966   80

Horowitz, Harold W. and Neitring, Diana L.
Equal protection aspects of inequalities in public education

and public assistance programs from place to place within a
state. UCLA Law Review 15: 787-816, April 1968   <u>81</u>
   Inequalities in educational opportunity
   among school districts within a state,
   p. 804-12.

Johnson, Virgil K.
   Inequality in tax assessments--multi-county school districts
   and new emphasis to an old problem. South Dakota Law Review
   11: 119-31, Winter 1966   <u>82</u>

Kirk, Russell
   Taxes and equality in schools. National Review 24: 287,
   March 12, 1972   <u>*83</u>

Michelman, Frank I.
   On protecting the poor through the Fourteenth Amendment.
   Harvard Law Review 83: 7-59, November 1969   <u>84</u>

National Committee for Support of the Public Schools
   School finance: a matter of equal protection? special report by Marian F. Bendixsen. 8p Washington, D.C., February
   1970   <u>*85</u>

A new study of the relation of the financial variables to educational quality. IAR Research Bulletin (Institute of Administrative Research, Teachers College, Columbia University) 11: 9-10, November 1970   <u>86</u>

Schoettle, Ferdinand P.
   The equal protection clause in public education. Columbia
   Law Review 71: 1355-419, December 1971   <u>87</u>

Shanks, Hershel
   Equal education and the law. American Scholar 39: 255-69,
   Spring 1970   <u>88</u>

Silard, John
   Alternative legislative options for achieving public educa-
   tion equalization. Compact (Education Commission of the
   States) 5: 40-41, December 1971   <u>*89</u>
      Concerning abandonment of the local prop-
      erty tax base for education; major shift
      of funding burden from local to state
      sources; power equalizing; local tax-
      yield equalization.

Silard, John and White, Sharon
   Intrastate inequalities in public education; the case for
   judicial relief under the equal protection clause. Wisconsin Law Review (1): 7-34, 1970   <u>90</u>

U.S. Advisory Commission on Intergovernmental Relations
Equalizing educational opportunity--the state, federal roles;
by John Shannon. In U.S. Senate Select Committee on Equal
Educational Opportunity, Equal educational opportunity, hearings, September 1970, pt. 7, p. 3551-58   *91

U.S. Federal Reserve Bank of Boston
Existing disparities in public school finance and proposals
for reform; by Steven J. Weiss. 140p (Research report no.
46) Boston, February 1970   *92
        Bibliography, p. 136-40.
Reprinted: U.S. Senate Select Committee on Equal Educational
Opportunity, Equal educational opportunity--1971, hearings,
pt. 16D-2, p. 7789-954
Excerpt: Need for change in state public school finance systems. New England Economic Review, January-February 1970:
3-22

U.S. Office of Education
Equality of educational opportunity; by James S. Coleman and
others. 737p (OE-38001) Washington, D.C., 1966   *93
        Summary of inequalities in school
        characteristics, p. 120+.
Comment: Toward open schools, by James S. Coleman. Public
Interest (9): 20-27, Fall 1967
Comment: The evaluation of equality of educational opportun-
ity, by James S. Coleman. 40p (P-3911) Santa Monica, Rand
Corporation, August 1968
Comment: The poor, the schools, and equal protection, by
David L. Kirp. Harvard Educational Review 38: 635-68, Fall
1968
Comment: Social class and equal educational opportunity, by
Alan B. Wilson. Harvard Educational Review 38: 77-84, Win-
ter 1968
Comment: A reappraisal of the most controversial educational
document of our time: the Coleman report, by Christopher
Jencks. New York Times Magazine, August 10, 1969: 12-13+

Urban Coalition
First annual report. 40p Washington, D.C., 1968   *94
        Membership of Task Force on Educational
        Disparities, p. 28.

Urban Institute
Local disparities at issue. Its Search 1:1, November-December 1971   *95

Public school financing; seeking ways to get more revenue
and more equitable distribution. Its Search 1:1, May-June
1971   *96

Urban Institute
  Unraveling state-local public school finance. Its Search
  1: 3-5, November-December 1971   *97

Walker, Mabel
  Fiscal problems of fractionated governments; with special
  reference to property taxation. Tax Policy (Tax Institute
  of America) 38 (10-12), October-December 1971   *98
        Decisions relating to educational and
        tax disparities in financing education,
        p. 16-17.

Wise, Arthur E.
  Rich schools, poor schools; the promise of equal educational
  opportunity. 228p Chicago, University of Chicago Press,
  1968   99
        Bibliography, p. 215-19.

FINANCING OF LOCAL PUBLIC SCHOOLS

Local public schools are financed mainly by local property taxes, and have been for many years. However, American education is not working well for millions of children, according to the President's Commission on School Finance. In addition to statewide funding of local education, the Commission recommended that the federal government provide funds ($4.6-7.8 billion) over five years to assist states to make the transition from local to statewide school financing, that school districts be permitted to use some local taxes to supplement state funds for schools, and that local school boards be given wide latitude to use resources provided by the state to best meet the local needs and demands.

U.S. President's Commission on School Finance
Progress report. 61p March 22, 1971   100

Schools, people and money; the need for education reform; final report. 147p Washington, D.C., March 3, 1972   101
    Pt. 2, c. 5: Full state funding of elementary and secondary education;
    Pt. 2, c. 13: Exploring innovations (vouchers and performance contracts).
Recommendations: Education Commission of the States Bulletin 5: 3, April 1972
Recommendations: ACIR Interchange (U.S. Advisory Commission on Intergovernmental Relations) (72-2), April 28, 1972
Comment: School financing: a new way to foot the bill, by John Herbers. New York Times, March 12, 1972: 3E
Comment: U.S. News and World Report, March 20, 1972: 79
Comment: NACo News & Views (National Association of Counties) 4: 1+, March 24, 1972
Comment: School finance: a return to "state prominence," by Phyllis Myers. City 6: 6+, March-April 1972
Comment: The President's Commission on School Finance, by Norman Karsh. Compact 6: 3-6, April 1972

Economies in education; by Cresap, McCormick and Paget, Inc. 285p Washington, D.C., 1972   102

Fact book. 19p Washington, D.C., 1972   103

14

U.S. President's Commission on School Finance
The foundation program and education needs; by
Arthur E. Wise. 25p Washington, D.C., 1972   104

In search of a rational basis for measuring
disparities, a review of per-pupil expenditure
makeup; by Sigmund L. Sklar. 121p Washington, D.C., 1972   105

Population, enrollment and costs of public elementary and secondary education, 1975-1976 and
1980-1981; by Simat, Heilleisen and Eichner,
Inc. v.p. Washington, D.C., 1972   106

Preprimary education: needs, alternatives, and
costs, 1971-1980; by Education and Public Affairs. v.p. Washington, D.C., 1972   107

Problems of financing inner-city schools; by
Ohio State University Research Foundation.
60p Washington, D.C., 1972   108

A prototype national educational finance planning model; by Sigmund L. Sklar. 199p Washington, D.C., 1972   109

Public school finance: present disparities and
fiscal alternatives; by Urban Institute. 2v
Washington, D.C., 1972   110

Review of existing state school finance programs; by Thomas H. Jones. 2v Washington,
D.C., 1972   111

Selected staff studies in elementary and secondary school finance. 91p Washington, D.C.,
1972   112
    Includes: Performance contracting,
    education vouchers, and aid programs.

State-local revenue systems and educational
finance; by Advisory Commission on Intergovernmental Relations. v.p. Washington, D.C.,
1972   113

What state legislators think about school finance; an opinion survey of state legislature
education committee chairmen; by Educational
Testing Service and James C. Falcon. 159p
Washington, D.C., 1972   114

Materials relating to financing of local public schools include the following:

Aaron, Henry J.
Local public expenditures and migration effect [with parti-
cular reference to education]. Western Economic Journal 7:
385-90, December 1969   115
Abstract: Journal of Economic Literature 8: 708, June 1970

American Association of School Administrators
Education revenue sharing: an essential reform; by Charles
B. Saunders, Jr., before annual convention, February 16,
1972.   116
Reprinted: Congressional Record, March 21, 1972: E2812-14

American Council on Education
School finance; by Lee O. Garber and E. Edmund Reutter, Jr.
Its Yearbook of School Law, 1970: 153-203   117

School finance; by Lee O. Garber and Reynolds C. Seitz. Its
Yearbook of School Law, 1971: 159-200   118

Barlow, Robin
Efficiency aspects of local school finance. Journal of Political Economy 78: 1028-40, September-October 1970   119

Benson, Charles S.
The economics of public education. ed. 2   368p   Boston,
Houghton, 1968   120
       Bibliography, p. 349-52.

Berke, Joel S.
The current crisis in school finance: inadequacy and inequi-
ty. Phi Delta Kappan 53: 2-7, September 1971   *121
Reprinted: U.S. Senate Select Committee on Equal Educational
Opportunity, Equal educational opportunity--1971, hearings,
pt. 16D-1, p. 7453-58

A national perspective on the problems and prospects of educational finance; before Conference on Alternative Financing
of Education, North Kingstown, January 20, 1970.   *122
Excerpt: Newsletter (University of Rhode Island, Bureau of
Government Research) 13 (8), April 1972

Campbell, Alan K.
Inequities of school finance. Education Digest 34: 10-13,
April 1969   123

Center for Applied Research in Education
  Financing public elementary and secondary education; by Howard R. Jones. 116p New York, 1966   124
        C. 3: Guidelines for state school support;
        C. 4: Issues and problems in the adminis-
        tration of state support;
        C. 5: Local revenues in the financing of
        public schools;
        C. 6: State taxation for public schools;
        C. 7: The role of federal government in
        financing education.

Committee for Economic Development
  Resources for urban schools: better use and balance; edited
  by Sterling M. McMurrin. 146p (Supplementary paper no. 33)
  New York, 1971   *125
        Financing education for the urban disad-
        vantaged, by Henry M. Levin, p. 3-22;
        Accountability in education, by Leon
        M. Lessinger, p. 23-48.

Conference on Economic Progress
  Achieving nationwide educational excellence: a ten-year plan
  to save the schools; by Leon H. Keyserling. 92p Washington, D.C., December 1968   *126
        C. 5: Paying the bills;
        C. 6: Can America afford adequate
        education?

Council of Planning Librarians
  The school in the urban comprehensive plan: a partial bibliography; compiled by Charles W. Barr. 38p (Exchange bibliography no. 264) Monticello, Ill., February 1972   *127
        School-community financial relation-
        ships, p. 22-26.

Education and public policy; symposium edited by Jack Culbertson. Public Administration Review 30: 331-75, July-August
  1970   *128
        The financing of elementary and secondary
        education, by H. Thomas James, p. 371-75.

Financial crisis for public schools. U.S. News and World Report, November 8, 1971: 48-50   *129

Garvue, Robert J.
  Modern public school finance. 378p New York, Macmillan,
  1969   130
        Includes: State-local systems of public
        school financial support.

Gauerke, Warren E. and Childress, Jack R., eds.
Theory and practice of school finance. 437p Chicago, Rand
McNally, 1967   131
        C. 6: Local, state and federal financing
        of locally operated elementary and secon-
        dary schools.

Gittell, Marilyn, ed.
Educating an urban population. 320p Beverly Hills, Calif.,
Sage Publications, 1967   132

Grieder, Calvin
Public school financing must be overhauled. Nation's Schools
87: 10, May 1971   133

Guthrie, James W. and Wynne, Edward, eds.
New models for American education. 258p Englewood Cliffs,
N.J., Prentice-Hall, 1971   134
        C. 12: A new model for school finance
        (capital embodiment).

Hack, Walter G. and Woodard, Francis O.
Economic dimensions of public school finance; concepts and
cases. 292p New York, McGraw-Hill, 1971   135

Hey, Robert P.
Wanted: better method to finance schools; indirect sales
levy or more U.S. tax aid. Christian Science Monitor, January 3, 1972: 1+   136

Hillenbrand, Bernard F.
The school finance explosion! editorial. American County
38: 6, January 1972   *137

Howe, Harold, II
Financing schools: property tax is obsolete; anatomy of a
revolution. Saturday Review, November 20, 1971: 84-88+ 138

International Association of Assessing Officers
Expenditures for education compared to local governments'
capacity to pay. Assessors News Letter 34: 14-15, January
1968   139

James, H. Thomas
Emerging patterns of federal, state and local control of education. Tax Digest 46: 6-11, Fourth Quarter 1968   140

Johns, Roe L. and Morphet, Edgar L.
The economics and financing of education; a systems approach.
ed. 2 580p Englewood Cliffs, N.J., Prentice-Hall, 1969
        C. 8: State provisions for school support.   141

Kelly, James A.
Judicial reform of educational finance; before Institute for
Chief State School Officers, San Diego, August 5, 1971. *142
Reprinted: U.S. Senate Select Committee on Equal Educational
Opportunity, Equal educational opportunity--1971, hearings,
pt. 16D-1, p. 7459-64

Lawyers' Committee for Civil Rights Under Law
Status report on school finance reform; by R. Stephen Browning. 3p+ (mim) Washington, D.C,, April 14, 1972   *143

Lawyers' Committee for Civil Rights Under Law, Education Commission of the States and National Committee for Support of
the Public Schools
School finance reform: a directory of organizations; compiled by Peter Leyton. [50]p Washington, D.C., March
1972   *144

Lindholm, Richard W.
Financing public education and the property tax. American
Journal of Economics and Sociology 29: 33-47, January 1970
                                                       145

Lutz, Harley L.
Can the property tax be replaced? Wall Street Journal, February 9, 1972: 12   146

Maeroff, Gene I.
School districts: why they are inherently unequal. New York
Times, September 5, 1971: 7E   147

Morphet, Edgar L. and Jesser, David L., eds.
Emerging designs for education: program, organization, oper-
ation and finance. 240p New York, Citation Press, 1968
      The economics and financing of education,   148
by R. L. Johns, p. 193-239.

National Association of Manufacturers. Committee on Taxation
and Council of State Chambers of Commerce. Committee on
State Taxation, Federal Finance Committee
Meeting summary, April 5-7, 1972, Miami, Fla.   13p (mim)
New York, 1972   *149
      The court cases: implications for educa-
tion and tax burdens, by J. Lee Hamilton;
The value-added tax: a better method or
just higher taxes? by George Cline Smith.

National Clearinghouse for Legal Services
School financing materials: sources of further information.
5p (Clearinghouse no. 7458) Chicago, Northwestern University, School of Law, 1971?   150

National Committee for Support of the Public Schools
Education in the states; a planning chart book. 32p Washington, D.C., 1966   <u>151</u>

How to change the system; proceedings of the 8th annual conference, March 22-24, 1970. 116p Washington, D.C., 1970
     Performance contracting, by Charles   *152
     Blaschke;
     Total state funding for education, by
     John Shannon;
     A voucher system for education, by
     Christopher Jencks;
     The federal role in education reform,
     by James E. Allen, Jr.

Statement regarding necessary reforms in the present system
of financing public education.   *153
Reprinted: U.S. Senate Select Committee on Equal Educational
Opportunity, Equal educational opportunity--1971, hearings,
pt. 16D-3, p. 8286-90

National Education Association. Committee on Educational Finance
Dimensions in school finance; edited by John K. Norton.
273p Washington, D.C., 1966   <u>154</u>
     C. 4: Raising the funds--necessity of
     new orientations.

Financial status of the public schools. 43p Washington,
D.C., 1971   <u>155</u>

National conference on school finance; proceedings, 8, 1965-
13, 1970:   <u>156</u>
8: Trends in financing public education. 248p 1965
9: Local-state-federal partnership in school finance.
165p 1966
10: The challenge of change in school finance. 226p 1967
11: Interdependence in school finance: the city, the state,
the nation. 243p 1968
12: Fiscal planning for schools in transition. 273p 1969
13: A time for priorities: financing the schools for the
70's. 203p 1970

National Education Finance Project
Future dimensions for school financing; a response to demands
for fiscal equity in American education. 61p Gainesville,
Fla., 1971   *157
     Concerning the myth of equal education;
     a primer of education finance; variations

in fiscal capacity and effort; the federal
role; blue-prints for state educational
equality.
Reprinted: U.S. Senate Select Committee on Equal Educational
Opportunity, Equal educational opportunity--1971, hearings,
pt. 16D-3, p. 8292-354
Comment: Toward equity in school finance, by R. L. Johns.
American Education 7: 3-6, November 1971
Comment: Federal study hits school funding inequities.
National Civic Review 61: 41, January 1972

National Education Finance Project
[Reports.] 6v Bethesda, Md., ERIC Document Reproduction
Service, 1971   158
        V. 1: Dimensions of educational need, by
        Roe L. Johns and others. 242p 1969
        V. 2: Economic factors affecting the fi-
        nancing of education. 372p 1970
        V. 3: Planning to finance education.
        463p 1970
        V. 4: Status and impact of educational
        finance programs, by Roe L. Johns and
        others. 336p 1970
        V. 5: Alternative programs for financing
        education. 363p 1971
        V. 6: Personal income by school dis-
        tricts in the United States.

[Special studies.]   159
        No. 7: Financing public elementary and
        secondary school facilities in the United
        States, by W. Montfort Barr and others.
        373p Bloomington, Indiana University,
        School of Education, Bureau of Surveys
        and Administrative Studies, 1970
        No. 10: Fiscal capacity and educational
        finance: variations among states, school
        districts, and municipalities. 286p
        Madison, University of Wisconsin, De-
        partment of Educational Administration,
        1970
        No. 11: The relationship of school dis-
        trict reorganization to state aid dis-
        tribution systems. 2pts Minneapolis,
        Educational Research and Development
        Council of the Twin Cities Metropolitan
        Area, Inc., 1970

National Tax Association and Fund for Public Policy Research
    Proceedings of National Tax Association Seminar on balanc-
    ing our federal-state-local fiscal system, July 22-24, 1971.

National Tax Journal 24 (3), September 1971   *160
   State takeover of education financing,
   by Paul D. Cooper;
   Foreign experience with a value-added
   tax, by Edwin S. Cohen;
   Integrating a federal value-added tax
   with state and local sales levies, by
   Richard W. Lindholm.

Pauly, Mark V.
   Mixed public and private financing of education: efficiency
   and feasibility. American Economic Review 57: 120-30, March
   1967   161

Rand Corporation
   Theoretical models of school district expenditure determin-
   ation and the impact of grants-in-aid; by S. M. Barro. 76p
   (R-867-FF) Santa Monica, February 1972   162

School finance in the seventies: the prospect for reform. Phi
   Delta Kappan 51 (3), November 1969   163
            The constitutional challenge to inequi-
            ties in school finance, by Arthur E. Wise;
            The judicial assault on state school aid
            law, by August W. Steinhilber;
            Performance proposals for educational
            funding; a new approach to federal re-
            source allocation, by Leon M. Lessinger
            and Dwight H. Allen.

Shaffer, Helen B.
   Public school financing. Editorial Research Reports, January 26, 1972: 63-84   164

Tax Foundation
   Property taxation. 10p (mim) (Research bibliography no.
   37) New York, December 1969   *165

U.S. Advisory Commission on Intergovernmental Relations
   Fortieth meeting, White Plains, N.Y., October 7-8, 1971.
   Washington, D.C., 1971   *166
            Includes: Progress report on project for
            President's Commission on School Finance.

U.S. Department of Agriculture. Economic Research Service
   Alternatives to the property tax for educational finance;
   by Jerome M. Stam and Thomas F. Hady, before Seminar on the
   Crisis in Public School Finance, Resource Economics Committee of the Great Plains Agricultural Council, Lincoln, April 13, 1972. 26p Washington, D.C., 1972   167

U.S. Library of Congress. Congressional Research Service
The question of school finance; recent selected references.
16p (ditto) (LB 2514) (72-13 ED) Washington, D.C., January 19, 1972   168

U.S. Department of Health, Education and Welfare. Office of
Education
Public school finance programs, 1968-69; compiled by Thomas
L. Johns. 335p (OE-22002-69) Washington, D.C., 1969   169

Walker, Mabel
Major impacts on the property tax. Municipal Finance 43:
117-21, February 1971   *170
Reprinted: Tax Policy (Tax Institute of America) 38: 3-8,
March 1971

Webb, Harold V.
The case for a new realignment of financial responsibilities
for education. American School Board Journal 159: 29-31,
December 1971   171

Zimmer, John M.
Expenditures for public elementary and secondary education
in counties classified by the relative poverty status of
their rural populations. Journal of Farm Economics 49: 1204
-08, December 1967   172

STATE FINANCING OF LOCAL PUBLIC SCHOOLS

Constitutionally, education is the responsibility of state government, but it has traditionally been a local function. In the average school district, local government pays slightly more than one-half the cost and the state about 40 percent, with the remainder coming from federal funds. Local governments raise most of their own revenues--seven of every eight dollars--from the property tax. The state share of education funding varies from 8.9 percent in New Hampshire to 100 percent in Hawaii, which has a centralized state-financed and state-administered school system.

> U.S. Advisory Commission on Intergovernmental Relations
> Who should pay for public schools: report of the Conference on State Financing on Public Schools, May 20, 1971. 44p (M-69) Washington, D.C., October 1971   *173

Materials relating to state financing of local public schools include the following:

Allen, James E., Jr.
 Perspectives on school finance. Perspectives on Education (Columbia University, Teachers College) 4: 1-7, Spring 1971
                                                                     174

 The state, educational priorities and local financing. Integrated Education 6: 55-61, September-October 1968   175

Association of School Business Officials of the United States and Canada
 Alternatives to state apportionment programs; six other ways to finance schools; by Peter C. Cameron. Its School Business Affairs, March 1972: 61-62   176

Benson, Charles S.
 The cheerful prospect: a statement on the future of public education. 134p Boston, Houghton, 1965   177
     C. 6: The role of the states in financing education.

Bruno, James E.
 Achieving property tax relief with a minimum disruption of state programs. National Tax Journal 22: 379-89, September 1969   *178
 Reprinted: (Reprint no. 52) University of California, Los Angeles, Institute of Government and Public Affairs, 1969

Bruno, James E.
An alternative to the use of simplistic formulas for deter-
mining state resource allocation in school finance programs.
American Educational Research Journal 6: 479-500, November
1969   *179
Reprinted: (Reprint no. 56) University of California, Los
Angeles, Institute of Government and Public Affairs, 1970

Colman, William G.
School finance: a challenge and a change; editorial. National Civic Review 60: 540-41+, November 1971   *180
Reprinted: Congressional Record, December 11, 1971: S21469-
70

The coming change in the property tax [case for state financing of education]. Business Week, February 12, 1972: 50-54
                                                        181

Coons, John E. and Others
Educational opportunity: a workable constitutional test for
state financial structures. California Law Review 57: 305-
421, April 1969   *182
Reprinted: U.S. Senate Select Committee on Equal Educational
Opportunity, Equal educational opportunity--1971, hearings,
pt. 16D-2, p. 8151-265

Private wealth and public education. 520p Cambridge, Bel-
knap Press, 1970   183
Excerpt: Introduction: values in collision. Congressional
Record, January 18, 1972: E10-16

Reslicing the school pie. Teachers College Record 72: 485-
93, May 1971   184
Reprinted: U.S. Senate Select Committee on Equal Educational
Opportunity, Equal educational opportunity--1971, hearings,
pt. 16D-2, p. 8266-74

Dye, Thomas R.
Politics, economics and educational outcomes in the states.
Educational Administration Quarterly 3: 28-48, Winter 1967
                                                        185

Ecker-Racz, L. L.
The politics and economics of state-local finance. 242p
Englewood Cliffs, N.J., Prentice-Hall, 1970   186

Ecker-Racz, L. L. and McLoone, Eugene
The state role in financing public schools. Education Digest 34: 5-8, December 1968   187

Education Commission of the States
  Consequence for the '70's [of the Serrano decision]. Compact 6: 7-9, April 1972   *188

  Financing public education. Compact 2 (1), February 1968
      New proposal to combine state and local   *189
      funding [by Advisory Commission on In-
      tergovernmental Relations], p. 7.

  Full state funding of schools; by J. Alan Thomas and others.
  37p (mim) Denver, March 11, 1970   *190

  Implications of full state funding; by George J. Crawford.
  Compact 6: 26-28, April 1972   *191

  New directions for education? Compact 5 (1), February 1971
      New directions in education, by Wendell   *192
      H. Pierce;
      OEO experiments in education, by Thomas
      Glennan;
      RAND/HEW study of performance contract-
      ing, by George R. Hall and James P.
      Stucker;
      Gary, Indiana contracts for operation
      of entire school, by Gordon McAndrew;
      A contractor's viewpoint: Texarkana Year
      II, by Edmund Zazzera;
      Giving parents money for schooling, by
      Christopher Jencks.

  New state role in financing schools; by James B. Conant, before 2d annual forum. Compact 2: 41-43, August 1968   *193

  [1971 annual meeting, July 7-9, Boston; highlights.] Compact 5 (special issue), September 1971   *194
      Educational innovations--performance
      contracting and vouchers, p. 19;
      Will success spoil education, by Robert
      E. Merriam, p. 11-13.

  Public elementary and secondary school data, March 1972.
  Compact 6: 24-25, April 1972   *195

  School support in the future; by K. F. Jordan. Compact 6:
  10-12, April 1972   *196

  State financial takeover called for [in New York]; by John
  V. Lindsay, before New York State Association of City Councils, January 1970. Compact 4: 34, April 1970   *197

Hettich, Walter
Equalization grants, minimum standards, and unit cost dif-
ferences in education [particularly in Michigan and New
York]. Yale Economic Essays 8: 5-55, Fall 1968   198

Keppel, Francis
The necessary revolution in American education. 201p New
York, Harper and Row, 1966   199
  C. 5: The capacity of the states and
  national educational policy.

Kotin, Lawrence
Equal educational opportunity: the emerging role of the
state board of education. Boston University Law Review 50:
211+, Spring 1970   200

National Committee for Support of the Public Schools
Issues in school finance; broadening the base of state sup-
port. 6p (Know your schools fact sheet no. 8) Washington,
D.C., October 1966   *201
___. revised September 1967
Reprinted: Compact 2: 7, February 1968

Starting over again with state aid for schools; by Charles
S. Benson, before 6th annual conference, March 16, 1968.
3p (Special report) Washington, D.C., September 1968
        *202

National Education Association. Committee on Educational Fi-
nance
Planning for educational development in a planning, program-
ming, budgeting system; prepared by the State-Local Finances
Project, George Washington University. 46p Washington,
D.C., 1968   *203

National League of Cities
National municipal policy, adopted at the 48th annual Congress of Cities, November 28-December 1, 1971. 92p Washington, D.C,, 1972   *204
  "As a long range objective, states should
  assume from local school districts the responsibility for raising funds to support
  public schools."

Peck, John E.
Economic argument for the state support of schools. School
Management 15: 36+, April 1971   205

How much state support for local schools? School Management
15: 6-7+, August 1971   206

Riew, John
    State aids for public schools and metropolitan finance. Land
    Economics 46: 297-304, August 1970   *207
        Concerning study of Milwaukee metropol-
        itan area.

Shannon, John
    State-local tax systems: proposals and objectives; before
    National Conference on Government of National Municipal
    League, November 15, 1971. National Civic Review 41: 170-
    79, April 1972   *208
        "The distinct possibility that states may
        have to assume most of the responsibility
        for financing local schools now stands out
        as the second major working force for major
        overhaul of the state-local revenue system."

Thomas, J. Alan
    Full state funding of education. Administrator's Notebook
    (University of Chicago, Midwest Administration Center) 18:
    1-4, May 1970   209

U.S. Advisory Commission on Intergovernmental Relations
    Fiscal balance in the American federal system. II: Metropol-
    itan fiscal disparities. 393p (A-31) Washington, D.C.,
    October 1967   *210
        Recommended changes in state school aid
        formula to reduce educational disparities.

    New proposals for 1970; ACIR legislative program. v.p. (M-45)
    Washington, D.C., July 1969   *211
        Includes: State financing of public
        elementary and public schools.

    1970 cumulative; ACIR state legislative program. v.p. (M-48)
    Washington, D.C., August 1969   *212
        Includes: State financing of public schools.

    New proposals for 1969; ACIR state legislative program.
    v.p. (M-39) Washington, D.C., June 1968   *213
        Includes: Metropolitan educational equali-
        zation authority.

    1968 state legislative program. 629p (M-35) Washington,
    D.C., September 1967   *214
        Includes: Fiscal measures for equalizing
        educational opportunities for economically
        and socially deprived children.

U.S. Advisory Commission on Intergovernmental Relations
1967 state legislative program. 60lp (M-33) Washington,
D.C., September 1966   *215
        Includes: Fiscal measures for equalizing
        educational opportunities for economically
        and socially deprived children.

The sources of financing for selected state and local government functions: education.... 16p (process) Washington, D.C., April 1968   *216

State aid to local government. 105p (A-34) Washington,
D.C., April 1969   *217
        Includes: State assumption of substantially
        all fiscal responsibility for financing lo-
        cal schools.
Reprinted: U.S. Senate Select Committee on Equal Educational
Opportunity, Equal educational opportunity--1971, hearings,
pt. 16D-3, p. 8413-528

State and local finances; significant features 1967 to 1970.
183p+ (M-50) Washington, D.C., November 1969   *218
        Table 4: Per capita amounts...state and
        local government finances, by state, 1967-
        68 (general expenditures for education).

State-local finances; significant features and suggested
legislation. 420p (M-74) Washington, D.C., 1972   *219
        State financing of public elementary and
        secondary schools; percentage increase
        in state taxes required for state financ-
        ing of 90% of public school costs, by
        state, p. 404-07.

State-local revenue systems and educational finance; a report presented to the President's Commission on School Finance. v.p. (process) Washington, D.C., November 12, 1971
        C. 1: State-local revenue systems and   *220
        educational finance;
        C. 2: The present state-local revenue
        system;
        C. 3: Achieving a heavy-duty state-
        local revenue system;
        C. 4: A high quality state-local revenue
        system (the role of the judges in pro-
        moting state-local fiscal reform).
        Appendix B: Bibliography.

U.S. Congress. Senate. Republican Policy Committee
State and local finances; some selected statistics. 20p
(Memo no. 72-4) Washington, D.C., February 17, 1972   *221

U.S. Department of Health, Education and Welfare
State variations in support of public schools; by Eugene P.
McLoone and Forrest W. Harrison. Its Health, Education and
Welfare Indicators Monthly, May 1965: 21-34   222

U.S. Federal Reserve Bank of Kansas City
State and local property taxation; by James R. Ukockis. Its
Monthly Review, February 1968: 3-10   *223

Arizona

Billings, R. Bruce
How Arizona shares tax revenues with school districts. Ari-
zona Review (University of Arizona, College of Business and
Public Administration) 20: 11-17+, December 1971   *224
        Table 2: Alternate school aid formulas:
        impact on hypothetical districts.

Arkansas

Arkansas. Legislative Council. Research Department
Review of recent efforts in the various states to promote
equity in property taxes. 30p (mim) (Informational memorandum no. 143) Little Rock, December 1, 1970   *225
        Includes: Capsule comparison of state and
        local support of public schools, 1968-69.

California

Benton, E. Maxwell
The 1969 state school support act. Tax Digest 47: 1-11,
Fourth Quarter 1969   226

        State school support and the 1967 Legislature. Tax Digest
        45: 1-19, Fourth Quarter 1967   *227

California. Advisory Commission on Tax Reform
Limits and burdens of taxes in California; by Bruce T. McKim.
31p (Researcher's tentative report) Sacramento, November
1968   *228

        Tax reform report. 62p (process) Sacramento, March 1969
        Recommended a statewide property tax   *229
        for public school purposes to overcome
        disparities of tax burden between dis-
        tricts.

California. Council on Intergovernmental Relations
Alternative fiscal models for tax and revenue sharing in
California; a report. 28p Sacramento, January 1969 *230
        Recommended a statewide property tax on

nonresidential property for elementary,
high school and junior college levels
and returned to districts on an equalization formula.

California. Department of Education. Division of Public School
Administration
Recommendations on public school support; a report to the
State Board of Education. 94p (process) Sacramento, March
1967   *231
     C. 12: Local property tax relief.

Structure of public school support and recommendations for
improvement; by Ray H. Johnson and Edwin H. Harper. 52p
Sacramento, 1969   *232

California. Department of Education. State Board of Education.
School Support Committee
Recommendations for public school support. 16p (mim) Sac-
ramento, March 1, 1972   *233

California. Department of Education. State Board of Education.
Statewide Council on Long-range School Finance Planning
Recommendations for public school support. 15p+ (process)
Sacramento, February 11, 1971   *234

California. Department of Education. State Committee on Public
Education
Citizens for the 21st century: long range considerations for
California elementary and secondary education; a report to
the California State Board of Education, May 23, 1968. 485p
(process) Sacramento, 1969   *235
     C. 13: Issues in financing education.

California. [Department of Finance]. Tax Research Group
     California tax study. 2pts Sacramento, January 1966   *236
     Pt. 1: State taxes.
     Pt. 2: Property taxes.

California. Governor
     [Tax reform program, proposed to the Legislature.] v.p.
     (mim) (News release #300) Sacramento, May 17, 1972   *237
          Provides 50-50 state-local financing of
          the basic education program.

California. Governor's Commission on Educational Reform
     Report. 70p Sacramento, January 1, 1971   *238
          Recommended a statewide tax on all real
          estate and personal property to finance
          the educational program of each school
          district.

California. Legislative-Executive Tax Study Group
   Preliminary report. 111p (process) Sacramento, November
   14, 1969   *239

California. Legislature. Assembly. Committee on Education
   Final report on education legislation, 1970 regular legislative session. 19p (process) Sacramento, September 1970
       School finance, p. 3-5.   *240

California. Legislature. Assembly. Committee on Revenue and
   Taxation
   Facts about the Watson initiative; a preliminary report; by
   Stephen E. Dykes. 23p+ (process) Sacramento, December 26,
   1971   *241
           Among other things, the initiative would
           shift education costs for grades K-12, in
           excess of a $2 local property tax, and total
           cost of community colleges to the state.

   Transcript, hearings on the Governor's tax reform message
   of April 8, 1969, [held] May 5-12, 1969. 116p+ (process)
   Sacramento, 1969   *242

California. Legislature. Assembly. Interim Committee on Education. Subcommittee on School Finance
   Report. 65p (Assembly interim committee reports, 1963-
   1965, v. 10, no. 18) Sacramento, January 1965   *243
   Same: California Legislature, Appendix to the Journal of
   the Assembly, v. 2, 1965

California. Legislature. Assembly. Interim Committee on Revenue and Taxation
   A program of tax reform for California, a major tax study,
   pt. 12. 376p (Assembly interim committee reports, v. 4,
   no. 19) Sacramento, July 1965   *244
           Includes: School property tax relief;
           reform in school apportionment formula.

California. Legislature. Constitution Revision Commission
   Article IX [education]: background study. 95p (process)
   Sacramento, March 17, 1967   *245
   _____Supplement, no. 1-5. May-December 1967

California. Legislature. Joint Legislative Budget Committee.
   Office of the Legislative Analyst
   Excess cost to school districts resulting from low income
   target areas, January 6, 1971. 31p (process) Sacramento,
   1971   *246

California. Legislature. Joint Legislative Budget Committee.
Office of the Legislative Analyst
Final summary of legislative and executive action on the budget bill and other measures with fiscal implications, 1971
session. 124p Sacramento, January 3, 1972   *247
        Assistance to local education, p. 93-104.

Implications of a statewide property tax with respect to
equalizing educational support; report to Senate Fact Finding Committee on Education [hearing in Los Angeles, September 8-9, 1966]. 29p (mim) Sacramento, 1966   *248
        Concerning wide variation in assessed
        valuation per pupil among state's school
        districts.

A preliminary analysis of the Governor's tax reform program.
19p (process) Sacramento, May 1, 1969   *249

Property tax and expenditure controls in local school districts (report to the 1970 regular session of the Legislature pursuant to Chapter 784, 1969, AB 606-Veysey). 43p
(process) Sacramento, January 12, 1970   *250

Public school finance. 5pts (mim) Sacramento, October 31,
1967   *251
        Pt. 1: The state school fund: expenditures
        for education;
        Pt. 2: The state school fund: its derivation
        and distribution;
        Pt. 3: The foundation program;
        Pt. 4: Glossary of terms most often used in
        school finance;
        Pt. 5: Current issues in educational finance.

California. Legislature. Senate. Fact Finding Committee on
Education
Proceedings of hearing: statewide property tax, Los Angeles,
September 8-9, 1966. 295p (process) Sacramento, 1966 *252

Report. 51p Sacramento, 1967   *253
        C. 5: Statewide property tax.
Same: California Legislature, Appendix to the Journal of
the Senate, Regular Session, v. 1, 1967

California. Legislature. Senate. Fact Finding Committee on
Revenue and Taxation
State and local fiscal relationships in public education in
California; by Charles S. Benson and others. 72p Sacramen-
to, March 1965   *254
Same: California Legislature, Appendix to the Journal of
the Senate, Supplement, v. 1, 1965

California. University, Los Angeles. Institute of Government
and Public Affairs
Fiscal outlook analysis for education; by Werner Z. Hirsch,
before International Future Research Conference, Kyoto,
April 1970. 20p (mim) (MR-140) March 1970   *255

Measurement of state effort to support public education; by
Marvin C. Alkin, before Committee on Educational Finance,
National Education Association, April 6, 1965. 22p (MR-38)
1965   *256
    Bibliography, p. 19.

California Chamber of Commerce
[Call for the state to split the cost of education with local school districts on a 50-50 basis; by George Moscone, before sixth annual statewide Tax Forum.] Pacific Business
Bulletin 62: 1+, April 3, 1972   *257

Constitutional law--equal protection--school financing system
that substantially relies on local property tax violates
equal protection clause. Vanderbilt Law Review 24: 1265-
73, November 1971   258

Cox, Ronald W.
Equal educational opportunity--the financial aspects. Tax
Digest 46: 23-27, First Quarter 1968   *259

School finance proposals. Tax Digest 47: 8-17, Second Quarter 1969   260

Governor [Ronald] Reagan and Speaker [Bob] Moretti again back
rival tax-school finance plans. California Journal 3: 144-
45, May 1972   *261

Greene, Leroy
School financing (California). Compact (Education Commission of the States) 5: 35-36, December 1971   *262

League of Women Voters of California
A brief history of education in California. 13p (process)
San Francisco, January 1972   *263

Money for schools--when? how? Its California Voter 17: 1-2,
April 1972   264

School facts, structure and financing of California's public schools. 14p San Francisco, January 1965   *265

Lindman, Erick L.
Financing public schools. Tax Digest 45: 23-26, First Quarter 1967   *266

Los Angeles Bureau of Municipal Research
    Opposing statewide property taxes for schools. Its Tax Talk
    (2009): 1-2, April 17, 1971   *267

    Supreme Court "clout" to the Legislature. Its Tax Talk
    (2028): 1-2, August 28, 1971   *268

Shannon, Thomas A.
    Survey of 1967 proposals for financing California schools.
    Tax Digest 45: 19-22, First Quarter 1967   *269

Statewide property tax for schools. California Journal 2: 72-
73+, March 1971   *270

Urban Institute
    Paying for public schools; issues of school finance in Cali-
    fornia; by Betsy Levin and others. 63p Washington, D.C.,
    April 1972   *271
    Comment: California: the challenge of school financing.
    Search 2 (2): 3-5, March-April 1972

Wicklander, Edgar B.
    The state school fund and the sales and use tax. California
    Education 3: 18, January 1966   *272

Colorado

Colorado. Legislative Council
    State aid to schools in Colorado. 366p (Research publica-
    tion no. 117) Denver, November 1966   *273

    State and local finance. 73p (process) (Research publica-
    tion no. 180) Denver, December 1971   *274
        The public school foundation act, p. 1-11.

Colorado Public Expenditure Council
    Colorado's property tax relief fund. Its Colorado Taxpayer
    Report 13: 1-6, March 17, 1967   *275
        "Added revenue for local schools resulting
        from the Property Tax Relief Fund served
        mainly to spur added spending."

Connecticut

Connecticut. Commission to Study the Necessity and Feasibility
    of Metropolitan Government
    The state's biggest business... policy papers. 348p Hart-
    ford, January 1967   *276
        Education--a responsibility of the state,
        by Niilo Kaponen, p. 133-43.

Connecticut. General Assembly. Interim Committee on Education
    Report. 87p Hartford, 1971   *277

Connecticut. State Revenue Task Force
    Report...to the Governor and General Assembly, February 11,
    1971. 45p+ Hartford, 1971   *278
        Includes: State aid to the localities
        (education).

Connecticut. University. Institute of Public Service
    Toward a state-local tax policy for Connecticut; by Patricia
    Stuart. Its Connecticut Government 25 (2), Winter 1971
    "Compelling though the arguments for state   *279
    assumption of education costs may be, the
    critical fiscal question still remains:
    how will revenue be collected at the state
    level to meet this expenditure?"

Connecticut Public Expenditure Council, Inc.
    Local public school expenses and state aid in Connecticut,
    school years 1966-67 through 1970-71. 32p Hartford, Janu-
    ary 1972   *280

Florida

Constitutional law--financing public education under the equal
    protection clause [Millage Rollback Act of 1969]. Univer-
    sity of Florida Law Review 23: 590-97, Spring 1971   281

Constitutional law--Florida limitation on local property tax
    rate for education violates equal protection [Millage Roll-
    back Act]. Duke Law Journal, October 1970: 1033-39   282

Florida. Department of Education. Division of Research
    The Florida public school finance program, 1968-69; by Marie
    A. Kohler. (Research report no. 66) Tallahassee, Septem-
    ber 1968   283

Florida. Legislature. House. Appropriations Committee
    A "fair share" plan for Florida schools; by Clem Lausberg.
    40p+ (process) Tallahassee, January 1971   *284

Florida. Legislature. Legislative Intern Program
    A strategy for the '70's in Florida public school finance;
    by Clem Lausberg. 71p (process) Tallahassee, October 1969
                                                                  *285

Georgia

George, W. Elmer
    Why property tax relief? Urban Georgia (Georgia Municipal

Association) 21: 10-12, December 1971   *286
Concerning a property tax relief proposal
by Association of County Commissioners and
Georgia Municipal Association.

Hawaii

Hawaii. University. Legislative Reference Bureau
Hawaii constitutional convention studies. 179p (process)
Honolulu, July 1968   *287
    Includes: Article IX: Education (Public).

Idaho

Idaho. Legislature. Interim Tax Study Committee
Report. 222p Boise, November 6, 1968   *288
    Report on the Idaho property tax system,
    by Max P. Arnold and Patrick C. McMahon,
    p. 111-200.

Illinois

Council of the Great City Schools
[Address on Chicago schools; by Mrs. Louis A. Malis, before
Fall conference, Minneapolis, November 12, 1971.]   *289
Reprinted: U.S. Senate Select Committee on Equal Educational
Opportunity, Equal educational opportunity--1971, hearings,
pt. 16D-3, p. 8590-601

Illinois. Constitution Research Group
Con-con; issues for the Illinois Constitutional Convention;
papers edited by Victoria Ranney. 512p Urbana, University
of Illinois Press, 1970   *290
    C. 17: Education, by Orville Alexander.

Illinois. Governor
Special message on elementary and secondary education; by
Richard B. Ogilvie, March 2, 1971. 11p Springfield, 1971
                                                         291

Illinois. Legislative Council
Formulas for state aid to local schools: II. 16p (Explor-
atory research memoranda, File 6-944 and File 7-503) Springfield, November 1969   *292

Illinois. Northern Illinois University. Center for Government-
al Studies
Governing Illinois under the 1970 constitutions; edited by
David R. Beam. 58p DeKalb, 1971   *293
    Revenue and finance, by James M. Bano-
    vetz, p. 31-35.

Illinois. School Problems Commission No. 8
Illinois school problems; report. 83p (process) Springfield, 1965   *294
      Includes: School finance.

Illinois. School Problems Commission No. 9
Illinois school problems; report. 67p (process) Springfield, 1967   *295
      Includes: State involvement in financing
      education.

Illinois. School Problems Commission No. 10
Illinois school problems; report. 79p (process) Springfield, 1969   *296
      Includes: Alternatives in educational
      expenditure policy for the state.

Indiana

Indiana. Commission on State Tax and Financing Policy
Evaluation of the school state aid scheme in Indiana; by
Herbert J. Kiesling. 62p Indianapolis, January 1969   *297
      Appendix: The equalization of educa-
      tional outputs.

Financing of the public elementary and secondary schools in
Indiana; by John E. Peck. 73p Indianapolis, 1970   *298

Steps to tax reform in Indiana; recommendations. 10p Indianapolis, November 1970   *299
      School finance, p. 6-9.

Indiana. Legislative Council
Biennial report to the 96th General Assembly, 1969. 667p
Indianapolis, 1969   *300
      V. 2, p. 239-58: Committee to Study Alter-
      native Methods of Public School Finance.

Report of the General Education Study Committee. 50p (process) Indianapolis, 1971   *301
      State assumption of total current operating
      costs of Indiana public schools, p. 28-36.

Indiana. University. Bureau of Government Research
State support of public education in Indiana; by F. Jean-
nette Knoll. Its Indiana Public Affairs Notes 7: 1-6, May-
June 1965   *302

Indiana. University. School of Business. Division of Research
An analysis of the distribution of state funds for public

schools to local units of government; by John E. Peck. Indiana Business Review 46: 14-23, December 1971-January 1972
303

Indiana. University. School of Business. Division of Research
The implications of change in the current method of financing education; by Saul Pleeter. Indiana Business Review
47: 10-15, February-March 1972   304

State aid to local education in Indiana: is it accomplish-
ing its intended purpose? by Edward G. Boehne. Indiana Business Review 43: 6-11, September-October 1968   305

Iowa

Iowa. Governor's Conference on Education
Proceedings, Des Moines, October 7-8, 1969. 312p Des
Moines, Office of Planning and Programming, 1969   *306
      Passing the bucks: who will pay? p. 285-
      309.

Iowa [Legislature] reforms school aid. State Government News
(Council of State Governments) 14: 6, August 1971   *307
      Concerning a foundation plan of school aid
      effective with 1972 school year.

Iowa. Taxation Study Committee
Final report. 28p (process) Des Moines, January 1971 *308
      Recommended establishment of foundation
      grant program.

Iowa. University. Institute of Public Affairs
Technical appendix to Iowa local governmental finance studies. 62p (process) Iowa City, 1965   *309
      Includes: Local and county school district
      levies.

Serrano v. Priest in Iowa: financing public education under
the Fourteenth Amendment. Iowa Law Review 57: 378-411, December 1971   310

Tax Research Conference, Sioux City
School taxes, 1973; tax reform gone sour. 5p (Comments no.
53) February 23, 1972   *311
      "Property tax relief promised in 1971 by
      new school-financing legislation 'more
      apparent than real.'"

Kansas

Kansas. Legislative Coordinating Council
  1971 reports and recommendations of the special, standing
  and subcommittees to the 1972 Legislature, filed with the
  Council. 819p Topeka, December 1971   *312
        Financing school districts, by Special
        Committee on School Financing, p. 124-28.

Kansas. Legislature. Joint Committee on School Finance
  Report. In Journal of the Senate, January 13, 1971   313

Kansas. Legislature. Joint Committee on the State Tax Structure
  Final report and recommendations, v. 1. 102p Topeka, January 1970   *314
        Committee did not find acceptable solu-
        tion to problem of joint school district
        levies where county assessment levels vary.

Kansas. Legislature. Special Committee on Assessment and Tax-
  ation
  Report and recommendations to the 1972 Legislature. 94p
  Topeka, December 1971   *315
        One aspect of school district income
        tax, p. 57-59.

Ridenour, Philip and Patricia
  Serrano v. Priest: wealth and Kansas school finance. University of Kansas Law Review 20: 213-26, Winter 1972   316

Kentucky

Kentucky. Legislative Research Commission
  Legislative report: National Education Association hearings;
  transcript of proceedings, Louisville, November 11-13, 1970.
  598p (process) (Informational bulletin no. 87) Frankfort,
  December 1970   *317

  State and local taxes; prepared by Tax Research Center, Western Kentucky University. 108p (Research report no. 44)
  Frankfort, December 1967   *318
        Includes: Inter-county differences in
        general revenue.

  State support to education. 24p (Memorandum no. 343) Frankfort, September 25, 1970   *319

Kentucky. University. Center for the Study of State and Local
  Government Economics
  Some problems of equity and adequacy in Kentucky's state-

local taxation; by Don M. Soule and Stephen E. Lile. 66p
(process) (Publication no. 1) Lexington, February 1970
*320

Kentucky. University. Office of Development Services and Bus-
iness Research
Changing directions in Kentucky school finance; by Wayne K.
Talley and Don M. Soule. 23p Lexington, August 1971 *321

National Education Association. Commission on Professional
Rights and Responsibilities
Kentucky: education in Kentucky; a legacy of unkept promise.
141p (Report of an investigation) Washington, D.C., May
1971
        Kentucky's school finance effort, p. 46-
    117.
Excerpt: U.S. Senate Select Committee on Equal Educational
Opportunity, Equal educational opportunity--1971, hearings,
pt. 16D-2, p. 8062-73

Stephenson, Jack G. and Richard C.
Public schools: Serrano v. Priest--a challenge to Kentucky.
Kentucky Law Journal 60: 156-73, Fall 1971   323

Maine

Maine. Legislature. Legislative Research Committee
First summary report to 103d Legislature. 132p Augusta,
January 1967   *324
        Public school laws, p. 111-32.

Maine. University. Bureau of Public Administration
The three R's of property taxation: revitalization, reform
and relief; selected proceedings from the Maine Property
Tax Conference, September 9-11, 1968. 81p (State series
no. 7) Bangor, July 1969   *325
        Property tax relief issues, by F. John
        Shannon, p. 47-52.

Maryland

Maryland. Commission to Study the State's Role in Financing
Public Education
Maryland's obligation to its children for their education.
36p (process) Annapolis, February 1971   *326
        Commission considered full state funding,
        full equalization and a combination of
        full funding and equalization.

Maryland. [Legislative Council]
The need for a comprehensive study of the financing of public education in Maryland. 15p (process) Annapolis, October 1969   *327

Maryland. Study Commission on the State Tax Structure
[Final report.] 273p (process) Baltimore, January 4,
1971   *328
        Appendix II-B: 1975 expenditure projections
        (elementary and secondary education);
        Appendix VII: Utilization of the property
        tax in Maryland, by Ray D. Whitman.

Sensenbaugh, James A.
Maryland: a case story. Compact (Education Commission of
the States) 6: 22-23, April 1972   *329
        On July 1, 1971, Maryland assumed fiscal
        responsibility of all new school construc-
        tion in local school systems.

Young Democratic Clubs of Maryland
Platform, 1971; adopted September 1971.   330
Reprinted: Congressional Record, January 27, 1972: E563-66
        "Total equalization of education cannot
        become a reality until the state...as-
        sumes a greater fiscal responsibility
        for all public schools."

Massachusetts

Massachusetts. Advisory Council on Education
Inequalities of educational opportunity in Massachusetts: a
preliminary report; by Andre Daniere and others. 33p (process) Boston, July 31, 1967   *331

The state dollar and the schools; a discussion of state aid
programs in Massachusetts and promising reforms; by Charlotte Ryan. 24p (process) Boston, 1970   332

Massachusetts. Department of Education
Report of Subcommittee A, Equal Educational Opportunities
Committee. 12p Boston, December 1971   333

Massachusetts. Department of Education and U.S. Office of Education
Increasing the effectiveness of federal-state cooperation;
a special conference project, Washington, D.C., June 22-24,
1967. 21p Boston, November 1967   *334
        Cover title: Federal-state cooperation in
        American education.

Massachusetts. General Court. Senate
Tentative proposals for a master tax plan for the commonwealth. October 1970   *335
        Includes: State property tax; state sup-
        port of local public schools.
    Reprinted: U.S. Senate Select Committee on Equal Educational
    Opportunity, Equal educational opportunity--1971, hearings,
    pt. 16D-2, p. 7973-8014

Massachusetts. General Court. Special Commission Established
to Make an Investigation...Relative to Improving and Extend-
ing Educational Facilities in the Commonwealth
Report. 98p (House no. 3300) Boston, January 1965   *336
        Sec. 15: Finance.

Final report. 624p (House no. 4300) Boston, June 1965
        C. 19: Finance and fiscal policy.

Massachusetts. General Court. Special Commission to Develop a
Master Tax Plan...
Fourth report. 635p (Senate no. 1486) Boston, April 1971
        C. 8: Education expenditure.   *337

Massachusetts. Legislative Research Council
Report relative to state assumption of local education costs
and provision of equal educational opportunity. 209p (House
no. 5447) Boston, April 7, 1971   *338
        Bibliography, p. 177-86.

Michigan

Anderson, J. W.
The Michigan example: if we throw out the school tax, then
what? Washington Post, January 19, 1972   339
Reprinted: Congressional Record, January 20, 1972: E289
        Governor of Michigan would replace property
        tax with increase in personal income tax and
        with a value-added tax on manufacturers.

Bronder, Leonard
Detroit metropolitan school finances--the revenue problem.
National Tax Journal 19: 399-410, December 1966   *340
        Concerning dependence upon property tax
        for local support of schools.

Citizens Research Council of Michigan
Analysis of the Governor's educational reform proposals. 31p
(Memorandum no. 213) Detroit, November 1969   *341

An analysis of the Governor's proposals for financing ele-
mentary-secondary public school operating costs and a

comparison with the Democratic Party proposal. 33p (Memorandum no. 223) Detroit, March 1972   *342

Citizens Research Council of Michigan
  Public education in Michigan; background paper. Detroit,
  1969   *343
          No. 2: Expenditures for elementary-
          secondary public education in Michigan;
          No. 3: Michigan state-local general rev-
          enue structure and public school revenues;
          No. 4: Revenues for elementary-secondary
          public education in Michigan;
          No. 5: The impact of economic growth on
          revenues for public elementary-secondary
          education in Michigan;
          No. 6: The financial condition of local
          public school districts in Michigan;
          No. 14: Alternative methods of financing
          public elementary-secondary education in
          Michigan.

Michigan. Department of Education
  Michigan school finance study; summary report. 37p (mim)
  Lansing, 1967   *344
          Recommended additional emphasis on use of
          state financial aid for reducing inequal-
          ities in educational opportunity in Mich-
          igan.

  School finance and educational opportunity in Michigan; by
  J. Alan Thomas. 418p (Michigan school finance study) Lansing, 1968   345

Michigan. Executive Office. Bureau of Programs and Budget
  School finance reform in Michigan--1971. 191p (process)
  (Technical report C1b) Lansing, April 1972   *346
          Appendix: Special message to the Legis-
          lature on excellence in education--equity
          in taxation, by Governor William G. Mil-
          liken, April 12, 1971;
          Proposed recodification of the State
          School Aid Act, 1972, by State Depart-
          ment of Education.

Michigan. Governor
  Excellence in education--equity in taxation; special mes-
  sage to the Legislature, April 12, 1971. 9p+ (process)
  Lansing, 1981   *347

  Initiative petition amendment to the Constitution [proposing
  a prohibition upon the use of the local property tax for

public education operating purposes, except for specialized
purposes]; to be voted on November 7, 1972. 1p Lansing,
1971   *348

Michigan. Governor
   A revenue sharing program for equity and excellence in education. 12p (process) Lansing, November 1971   *349

Michigan. Governor's Commission on Educational Reform
   Report. 21p Lansing, September 30, 1969   *350
         Recommended a uniform, statewide property
         tax for school operating purposes to re-
         place local property taxes.
   Comment: Michigan Governor proposes state payment of school
   costs. National Civic Review 58: 491-92, November 1969

Michigan. Governor's Special Commission on Land Use
   Report. 30p (process) Lansing, January 5, 1972   *351
         Recommended that there be a shift from
         local property taxes as the major source
         of local government revenue.

Michigan. Legislative Fiscal Agency. Education Analysis Unit
   A dozen questions and answers about school aid; by James
   Wegryn. 19p (mim) Lansing, April 20, 1971   *352

Michigan. Office of Planning Coordination. Bureau of Policies
   and Programs
   An update of educational reform in Michigan. 150p (process)
   (Technical report D3a) Lansing, October 1970   *353

Milliken, William G.
   Quality education, the Constitution, and you. MASB Journal
   (Michigan Association of School Boards), January 1972: 18-20
                                                            *354

Phelps, James
   Explanation of Governor Milliken's proposed constitutional
   amendment to Article 9, Section 6. MASB Journal (Michigan
   Association of School Boards), January 1972: 20-21   *355

Urban Coalition
   Schools and inequality; by James W. Guthrie and others. 266p
   Washington, D.C., 1969   *356
         Bibliography, p. 253-66.
   Same: 266p Cambridge, Massachusetts Institute of Technology
   Press, 1971
   Same: U.S. Senate Select Committee on Equal Educational Op-
   portunity, Equal educational opportunity--1971; hearings,
   September 21-23, 28-30, October 1971, pt. 16C, Appendix I
   Summary: Educational inequality, school finance, and a plan

for the '70's. U.S. Senate Select Committee on Equal Educational Opportunity, Equal educational opportunity, hearings, September 1970, pt. 7, p. 3451-500

Minnesota

Anderson, Wendell R.
Minnesota's fiscal milestone [1971 tax reform]. Compact
(Education Commission of the States) 7: 19-21, April 1972
*357

Citizens League of Minneapolis and Hennepin County
State adopts historic changes in policy on local government;
Legislature assumes major responsibility for revenue "mix."
Its Citizen League News 20: 1+, November 18, 1971   *358
Reprinted: Congressional Record, December 11, 1971: S21470

Citizens League of Minneapolis and Hennepin County. Committee
on Revenue Distribution
New formulas for revenue sharing in Minnesota. 61p Minneapolis, September 1970   *359
          School finance, p. 20-25.

Citizens League of Minneapolis and Hennepin County. Fiscal
Disparities Committee
Breaking the tyranny of the local property tax: a proposal
to relate tax policy to urban development in the Twin Cities
Area. 32p (mim) Minneapolis, March 20, 1969   *360

League of Women Voters of Minnesota
Equality of educational opportunity. 48p St. Paul, February 1970   *361
          What is the state's role in providing
          equality of educational opportunity?

Metropolitan Council of the Twin Cities Area
The impact of fiscal disparity of metropolitan municipalities and school districts. 108p St. Paul, March 1971   *362
          Bibliography, p. 106-08.

State aids to public schools: their impacts and some proposals for reform; by O. H. Brownlee. 15p (mim) St. Paul,
July 1970   *363

Minnesota. Governor
Budget message to the Minnesota Legislature, 1971. 49p St.
Paul, 1971   364
          Recommended a new formula for determin-
          ing state aid.

Minnesota. Governor's Advisory Committee on Education for the
  Seventies
  Report and recommendations. 20p St. Paul, 1970   *365
      Finance, p. 7-11.

Minnesota. Governor's Property Tax Advisory Committee
  Report. 33p (process) St. Paul, December 14, 1970   *366

Minnesota. Legislature. Elementary and Secondary Education
  Commission
  Report. 21p St. Paul, January 15, 1969   *367
      Recommended that Legislature move toward
      goal of providing 50 percent of financial
      support for maintenance costs of elementary
      and secondary education.

Minnesota. State Planning Agency
  An analysis of the effects of the Minnesota Property Tax
  Reform and Relief Act on the financial positions of local
  governments; by O. H. Brownlee. 14p St. Paul, November
  1970   *368

  State aid to local government in Minnesota; by O. H. Brownlee. 16p St. Paul, November 1970   *369

Upper Midwest Research and Development Council
  Disparities caused by school district property tax bases in
  the Minneapolis-St. Paul seven-county metropolitan area; by
  David S. Dahl. 14p (process) Minneapolis, 1968   *370

Mississippi

Mississippi. Department of Education. Division of Administration and Finance
  Financing Mississippi public schools. 29p Jackson, 1971
                                                          371

Missouri

Missouri. School District Reorganization Commission
  School district organization for Missouri; a plan to provide equal access to educational opportunity for all children. 127p Jefferson City, November 1968   *372

St. Louis, Mo. Public Schools
  A tale of two cities: a blueprint for equality of educational opportunity in the St. Louis public schools. 93p March
  1968   *373
      Sec. 4: Who pays the piper?

Washington University. Institute for Urban and Regional Studies
Alternative measures of fiscal redistribution: gross v. net
aid; by David Barkin and John Legler. 14p (mim) (Working
paper EDA-9) St. Louis, April 1968   *374
        Concerning a grant-in-aid program for
        education in Missouri.

The equalizing impact of state aid to education; by David
Barkin. 22p (mim) (Working paper EDA-3) St. Louis, June
1967   *375
        Comparison of state aid programs in
        Kentucky, Missouri and Tennessee.

Nebraska

Governmental Research Institute, Inc., Lincoln
Federal aid to the Lincoln public schools. 11p (process)
(Bulletin v. 21, no. 13) June 1968   *376

State aid to the Lincoln public schools. 7p (process)
(Bulletin v. 21, no. 14) October 1968   *377

Nebraska. Legislature
[State assumption of most of the cost of financing public
schools approved by the Legislature, vetoed by the Governor
during 1972 session.] State Government News (Council of
State Governments) 15: 7, June 1972   *378

Nebraska. State Department of Education
State aid for Nebraska public school districts; general information. 2p (mim) Lincoln, 1967?   *379

Nevada

Nevada. Governor
Message to the Legislature, fifty-sixth session, 1971. 24p
Carson City, 1971   *380

Nevada. Legislative Counsel Bureau
State financial support for public schools. 64p (Bulletin
no. 69) Carson City, January 1967   *381

New Hampshire

New Hampshire. General Court. Fiscal Committee. Subcommittee
on Education
Report on study to determine if any relationship exists between educational excellence and educational cost in New
Hampshire public schools. 21p (process) Concord, May 14,
1968   *382

New Jersey

New Jersey. County and Municipal Government Study Commission
Beyond local resources: federal/state aid & the local fiscal crisis; fourth report. 38p Trenton, April 1971   *383
    Figure 8: Trend of school expenditures
    and state school aid, 1963 to 1971.
    ___; supplement. 74p July 1971

New Jersey. Governor's Welfare Study Commission
Report and recommendations. 32p+ (process) Trenton, January 1971   *384
    Education of children in disadvantaged
    areas, p. 31.

New Jersey. Legislature. Senate and Assembly Committees
Public hearing on S. B. 575, increased state aid for public
schools, June 9, 1970. 78,183p Trenton, 1970?   385

New Jersey. State Aid to School Districts Study Commission
A commitment to New Jersey's children; a state school support program for New Jersey; final report pursuant to P. L.
1966, c. 32. 126p (mim) Trenton, December 19, 1968 *386

Public hearing, Trenton, November 22, 1966-January 3, 1967.
3v (mim) Trenton, 1966-67   387

New Jersey. Tax Policy Committee
Report. 6pts Trenton, February 23, 1972   *388
    Pt. 2: The property tax;
    Pt. 3: State aids and service levels;
    Pt. 6: Summary.
Comment: New Jersey committee recommends drastic shift from
property tax. MFOA Newsletter (Municipal Finance Officers
Association of the United States and Canada) 47: 32, April
1, 1972

New Jersey Taxpayers Association
Financing New Jersey state and local government; the major
problem. 84p (process) Trenton, 1971   *389
    Recommended state taking increased respon-
    sibility for support of education.

Newark, N.J. Office of Economic Development
A blueprint for solving New Jersey's fiscal and tax problems:
a guideline for action for the state, for Newark and all
other municipalities in New Jersey; by P. Bernard Nortman.
41p (mim) June 1970   *390
    Concerning a broad based state income tax and
    assumption by the state of full cost of elemen-
    tary and secondary education.

New Mexico

Baggett, Bryce and Harris, Laurence
Directions to full state funding. Compact (Education Commission of the States) 4: 58-61, October 1970   *391

New Mexico. Educational Research Committee
State responsibility for public school education in New Mexico: a critical analysis and recommendations; final report.
96p   Santa Fe, June 1967   *392

New York State

Berke, Joel S. and Others
Equity in financing New York City's schools: the impact of
local, state and federal policy. Maxwell Review (Syracuse
University) 8: 9-25, Winter 1971-1972   393

Kelly, James A.
Resource allocation and educational need, New York City's
public schools. Education and Urban Society 2: 251-76, May
1970   394

New York State. Commission on the Quality, Cost and Financing
of Elementary and Secondary Education
Report. v. 1 v.p. (process) New York, 1972   395
        C. 2: School finance: toward equality of
        opportunity;
        C. 3: Federal aid to education.
Comment: N.Y. Commission [Fleischman Commission] urges state
school tax. National Civic Review 61: 148-49, March 1972
     396

New York State. Department of Audit and Control. Bureau of
Municipal Research and Statistics
State aid to local government, 1971. 131p Albany, Novem-
ber 1971   *397
        Education, p. 15-46.

New York State. Temporary State Commission on the Constitutional Convention
Education. 90p (Report no. 6) New York City, March 3,
1967   *398
        Bibliography, p. 88-90;
        Includes: State responsibilities for educa-
        tion; financial provisions for schools.

New York State. University of the State of New York. State
Education Department
The crisis in school finance; by Ewald B. Nyquist, before
Conference to Review the Findings and Recommendations of

the National Educational Finance Project, March 24, 1972.
7p (mim) Albany, 1972   399

New York State. University of the State of New York. State
  Education Department
  Full state funding and local school board policy-making; by
  Ewald B. Nyquist, before National School Boards Association,
  April 17, 1972. 14p (mim) Albany, 1972   400

New York State. University of the State of New York. State
  Education Department. Bureau of Educational Finance Research
  Analysis of school finances, New York State school dis-
  tricts, 1966-67; by David Billmyer. 44p (mim) Albany,
  February 1968   *401

  Analysis of school finances, New York State school districts, 1969-70.   *402
  Reprinted: U.S. Senate Select Committee on Equal Educational Opportunity, Equal educational opportunity--1971; hearings, pt. 16D-3, p. 8529-78
        C. 3: The impact of the New York State
        aid formula, 1961-62 to 1969-70.

  Measurement of the ability of local governments to finance
  local public services; by Lloyd L. Hogan. 102p Albany,
  1967   403
        Bibliography, p. 103-04.

  A review of operating expense proposals from the Report of
  the New York State Commission on the Quality, Cost and Financing of Elementary and Secondary Education. 15p (process) Albany, February 1972   404

  Studies of public school support, 1967 series: the urban
  education crisis--some fiscal considerations. 81p (process) Albany, February 1968   *405
        Includes: The general state aid formula;
        local fiscal ability; federal aid.

  Studies of public school support, 1968 series: studies of
  fiscal support, 1967-68 school year. 84p (mim) Albany,
  May 1969   *406
        Pt. B: The general state aid formula;
        Pt. D: Problems of measuring ability and
        needs.

  Understanding financial support of public schools, 1970-71;
  by Fred H. Bentley. ed. 2 38p (process) Albany, September 1970   *407

New York State. University of the State of New York. State
Education Department. Division of Educational Finance
Full state funding of elementary and secondary education in
New York State. 45p (mim) Albany, February 1972   408

New York State. University of the State of New York. State
Education Department. Information Center on Education
Annual educational summary, 1969-70. 195p (process) Al-
bany, 1970?   409

New York State Educational Conference Board
Background paper on state and local taxation; by Eugene Mc-
Loone. 23p (process) Albany, July 1969   *410

   Education for the seventies; a review of public school finance, 1969-1970. 55p Albany, September 1969   *411
          Includes: Intergovernmental relations in
          public school finance; fiscal structure
          for education; governmental structure for
          public school finance.

   Report on study of New York State school support formula
   staff study. 4nos (mim) Albany, 1969   *412
          No. 1: Intergovernmental relations in public
          school finance--1970, by Arvid J. Burke;
          No. 2: The fiscal structure for education, by
          John W. Polley;
          No. 3: Governmental structure for public school
          finance, by Robert L. Lorette and others;
          No. 4: Development of a measure of educational
          need and its use in a state school support form-
          ula, by Walter I. Garms and Mark C. Smith.

Pratt Institute. Department of City and Regional Planning
   Relieving real estate of school tax burdens in New York
   State; by George M. Raymond. 9p (Pratt planning papers)
   Brooklyn, N.Y., September 1970   *413
          Concerning transfer of total financial
          responsibility for support of public edu-
          cation to the state.
   Comment: Property tax: shifting the school burden, by George
   M. Raymond. Urban Land 30: 10-16, December 1971

Rochester Center for Governmental and Community Research, Inc.
   A county income tax for education? a report prepared for the
   Monroe County Educational Planning Committee; by Friedrich
   J. Grasberger. 57p (process) Rochester, N.Y., October
   1971   *414
   Comment: New York State Taxpayer (Citizens Public Expendi-
   ture Survey) 33: 7, January-February 1972

Westchester County, N.Y. Department of Planning
  School taxes and residential development. 87p White Plains,
  November 24, 1971   *415
    Includes: Alternate tax proposals.

North Carolina

Dees, John W.
  Serrano v. Priest; implications for financing public schools;
  is North Carolina's system of financing public schools constitutional? Popular Government (University of North Carolina, Institute of Government) 38: 3-12+, December 1971 *416

North Carolina. Governor's Study Commission on the Public
  School System
  Report. 303p Raleigh, December 1968   *417
  Condensed: A child well taught! the report. 36p Raleigh,
  1968
        Financial support for education, p. 16-18.

Ohio

Battelle Memorial Institute
  Local government tax revision in Ohio; research report to
  the state of Ohio; by John H. Bowman and others. 100p
  Columbus, January 4, 1968   *418
    Allocation among school districts, p. 73-75.

Governmental Research Institute, Cleveland
  State foundation support for Cuyahoga County school districts. 2p (process) (Governmental facts no. 145) February 22, 1968   *419

  State foundation support for the nine largest Ohio school
  districts. 2p (process) (Governmental facts no. 147)
  April 4, 1968   *420

Ohio. General Assembly. House. Bipartisan Select Committee on
  Tax Revision
  Framework for the future; information on the Sealy bill, a
  proposal for better financing of schools and local government. 13p Columbus, 1969   *421

Ohio. Legislative Service Commission
  Goals and practices in public education. 89p (Staff research report no. 73) Columbus, February 1965   *422
        State financial aid: the school founda-
        tion formula, p. 61-75.

  The Ohio school foundation program, and, Report of the Committee to Study the Ohio School Foundation Program. 64p

(Staff research report no. 94) Columbus, January 1969 *423
    Concerning state aid to elementary and
    secondary education.

PACE (Program for Action by Citizens in Education) Association
    Equalizing education through financial reform; considera-
    tions for future legislation; by Joel B. Stronberg. 15p
    Cleveland, 1972   *424
                Concerning state assumption of major
                burden of financing all levels of elementary
                and secondary education.

School financing in Ohio; a need to change; by Joel B. Stron-
    berg. 35p (process) Cleveland, 1971   *425
                Concerning a Serrano suit filed in Ohio
                federal district court, November 24, 1971.

Thatcher, George W.
    Financing education in Ohio. Miami Business Review (Miami
    University, Bureau of Business Research) 38: 1-4, April 1967
                                                            426

Toledo Area Governmental Research Association
    (formerly Greater Toledo Municipal League)
    Area school financing, 1969-1970. 5p (Report no. 150) To-
    ledo, March 1971   *427

    Per pupil valuation and school property tax rates, 13 area
    school districts, 1959-1968. 5p (Report no. 139) Toledo,
    December 1969   *428

    Property taxes and schools. 9p (Report no. 152) Toledo,
    September 1971, reprinted November 1971   *429

    School property tax rates, 1958-1969. 2p (Report no. 133)
    Toledo, April 1969   *430

    Toledo public schools--10 years to austerity. 12p (Report
    no. 153) Toledo, December 1971   *431

Oregon

Lindholm, Richard W. and Others
    Some notes on alternative proposals for property tax relief
    and tax reform in Oregon. Oregon Business Review (Univer-
    sity of Oregon, Bureau of Business and Economic Research)
    28: 1-9, January 1969   *432

Oregon. Department of Education. Division of Education Devel-
    opment
    Financing Oregon education: a statement prepared by the Gov-

ernor's Education Improvement Advisory Commission.   8p (process)   (Report no. 3)   Salem, 1965   *433
    Disparities in total tax burden among
    communities, p. 5.

Oregon. Governor
A description and analysis of Oregon's fiscal system: Area
21: primary and secondary education; by Richard W. Lindholm.
48p (process) Salem, January 1971   *434
    Bibliography, p. 46-48.

[School financing; by Tom McCall, before National School
Boards Association, April 17, 1972. 9p (mim) Salem,
1972   *435

Special message on report of Business Task Force on Education; by Tom McCall. 13p (mim) Salem, March 12, 1969
    Recommended revising the system for financ-   *436
    ing local school districts, and establishing
    a two-part funding system.

Oregon. Governor's Education Improvement Advisory Commission
Final report. 89p (process) Salem, 1966   *437
    Financing Oregon education, p. 23-29.

Oregon. University. Bureau of Governmental Research and Service
Selected data on the finances of state and local governments
in Oregon; by Evan Iverson and others. 55p (Finance bulletin no. 9) Eugene, April 1971   *438
    Includes: School districts.

Oregon. University. College of Education. School Study Council
Income vs. property: a new look at tax equity in Oregon
school finance; by Gregory S. Paus. 52p (mim) Eugene,
1971   *439
    Concerning use of income-based, ability-
    to-pay principle rather than ad valorem
    tax on property.

Pennsylvania

Committee of Seventy and Temple University
Assembly on Philadelphia's financial crisis, February 4-5,
1972.   440
Reprinted: Congressional Record, February 18, 1972: E1348-
52

Pennsylvania. Board of Education
1970 subsidy study. 25p+ (mim) Harrisburg, November 13, 1970   *441
    Appendix 1: Financing elementary and sec-
    ondary education in Pennsylvania, by
    J. Alan Thomas and others, October 1970.

Pennsylvania. Department of Education. State Intergovernmental
Education Project
Evidence for administrative changes in federal-state-local
education; by Edgar Fuller. 149p Harrisburg, 1971   442

Quinn, Pamela P.
Pennsylvania's state aid to education formula: a goal of
uniform equalized education. University of Pittsburgh Law
Review 30: 41-69, Fall 1968   443

Stafford, D. F.
State subsidy program. Pennsylvania School Journal 119: 84-
85, September 1970   444

U.S. Federal Reserve Bank of Philadelphia
The financial future of city and school government in Philadelphia; by David W. Lyon. Its Business Review, March 1971:
3-71   *445

Paving the school district's bumpy fiscal road. Its Business
Review, October 1971: 8-11   *446

State dollars to school districts; by Kathryn L. Kindl. Its
Business Review, June 1971: 3-11   *447

South Carolina

South Carolina. General Assembly. Committee to Study the Feasibility of Providing Additional Revenue for Educational Purposes
Report. 21p Columbia, 1969   *448

South Dakota

South Dakota. Legislative Research Council
The costs of elementary and secondary education in South Dakota; a compilation of data relevant to all common and independent school districts in the state on a county by county
basis. 68p (process) (Special report) Pierre, August 17,
1966   *449
____. rev.ed. 68p (process) (Special report) January 1,
1967

South Dakota. Legislative Research Council
  Effects of South Dakota's minimum foundation program. 38p
  (process) (Staff background memorandum) Pierre, July 20,
  1965   *450

  Municipal and rural property tax levy zones for school support. 20p (process) (Staff memorandum) Pierre, July 1,
  1965   *451
  ____; supplement no. 1. 7p (process) September 10, 1965

  School district reorganization: the 12 year district proposal and revenue sources for education. 98p (Staff memorandum) Pierre, July 27, 1966   *452

Texas

Texas. Committee on State and Local Tax Policy
  The Texas tax structure, 1970. 2nos Austin, November 1970
      1: The taxes we pay.   *453
      2: How our taxes compare.

Texas. Governor's Committee on Public School Education
  To make Texas a national leader in public education; the
  challenge and the chance; report. 76p Austin, August 31,
  1968   *454

  Public education in Texas--financing the system. 102p
  (process) (Research report v. 5, The challenge and the
  chance) Austin, 1969   *455
      Recommended a plan to equalize responsi-
      bility and effort.

Texas. Legislative Council
  State mineral income and the available school fund. 45p
  (Report no. 61-5) Austin, January 1971   *456

Texas. University. Institute of Public Affairs
  Elementary and secondary education aid: toward an optimal
  program for the state government of Texas; by Daniel C. Morgan, Jr., and Francis G. Hayden. 156p (Public affairs series no. 80) Austin, 1970   *457

Texas Research League
  Public school finance problems in Texas; an interim report.
  29p+ (process) Austin, June 1972   *458

Utah

Utah. Legislative council
  Report and recommendations, December 1970. 71p+ (process)

Salt Lake City, 1970   *459
    Recommended continuing study of school-
    finance formula.

Virginia

Moore, Hullihen W.
    In aid of public education: an analysis of the education
    article of the Virginia Constitution of 1971. Richmond Law
    Review 5: 263+, Spring 1971   460

Virginia. Commission to Study the Formula for State Aid to Pub-
    lic Schools
    A new plan; report. 42p (House document no. 20) Richmond,
    1970   *461
            Concerning the establishment by the General
            Assembly of the cost per student of a basic
            program of education; one-half of total state-
            wide cost to be paid by the state and one-half
            by localities, subject to such state additions
            as may be necessary.

Virginia. Division of State Planning and Community Affairs.
    Research Section. Staff
    Staff report to the Revenue Resources and Economic Study Com-
    mission; by John L. Knapp and others. 184p Richmond, 1970
            State assumption of financial responsi-   *462
            bility for education, p. 154-56.

Washington

Washington. Legislature. Joint Committee on Education. Subcom-
    mittee on School Finance
    General cash flow problems in school districts in the state
    of Washington: a report. 24p (mim) Olympia, November 12,
    1970   *463

    Proposed alterations of factors in the schools apportionment
    formula: a report. 47p (mim) Olympia, January 8, 1971
                                                             *464

    "Remote and necessary"; a special report [concerning dis-
    bursements of state funds to local school districts]. 28p
    Seattle, December 1, 1969   *465

Washington. Legislature. Legislative Budget Committee
    State support of public schools; report to the Legislature.
    210p (Report no. 66-9) Olympia, November 1966   *466
            Includes: State school support formulas;
            property tax; construction aid; trans-
            portation aid; federal aid to schools.

Washington. Legislature. Special Levy Study Commission
Education for the 1970s; facts and ideas assembled for citizens consideration.   47p   (mim)   Olympia, 1970   *467

Preliminary report.   35p   (process)   Olympia, January 1970

Summary report.   57p   Olympia, 1971
     Recommended greater state assumption of
     educational finance.

Summary report and research reports.   2v   (process)   Olympia,
March 1971
     Washington state education funding formula
     simulation study, v. 2, p. 1-256;
     Performance contracting arrives on the ed-
     ucation scene, v. 2, p. 421-31.

Washington. Superintendent of Public Instruction
Citizens' handbook on Washington public school administra-
tion and finance; by George M. Eisentrout.   28p   (process)
Olympia, March 1970   *468

Wisconsin

Rossmiller, Richard A.
The equalization objective in state support programs; an
analysis of measures need and ability.   National Tax Journal 18: 362-69, December 1965   *469
     Concerning study of 104 Wisconsin school
     districts during 1959-60.

State school aids--explanation of aid formulas used and amounts
paid to districts.   Wisconsin Taxpayer 33: 1-9, May 1965
                                                          *470

Wisconsin. Governor's Commission on Education
A forward look; final report.   84p+   (process)   Madison,
November 20, 1970   *471
     Financing public elementary and secondary
     education, p. 33-40.

Wisconsin. Task Force on Local Government Finance and Organization
Education research report.   11nos   Madison, 1968   *472
     No. 2: Wisconsin school aid formula, by
     C. K. Alexander and Bonnie Reese;
     No. 3: Excess aid payment districts, by
     C. K. Alexander and Bonnie Reese;
     No. 6: Flat and equalization aid districts,
     by C. K. Alexander and Bonnie Reese.

FEDERAL ASSISTANCE IN FINANCING LOCAL PUBLIC SCHOOLS

Until the 1940s it was accepted that responsibility for the lower levels of education rested in the state and local communities. In 1948, the United States Senate passed a general school aid bill. Not until 1960 did the House approve of the concept, and it was in 1965 that the first broad general aid bill was enacted and it focused on disadvantaged children. The Elementary and Secondary Education Act (Pub.L. 89-10) was approved April 11, 1965. Title I directed funds to school districts on the basis of the number of children from low-income families in the area.

> Congressional Quarterly, Inc.
>   Congress and the nation, v. 2, 1965-1968; a
>   review of government and politics during the
>   Johnson years. 974p+ Washington, D.C., 1969   *473
>   Federal education programs, p. 709-19.

Materials relating to federal assistance in financing local public schools include the following:

Bailey, Stephen K. and Mosher, Edith K.
  ESEA: the Office of Education ministers a law. 393p Syracuse, Syracuse University Press, 1968   474

Benton, E. Maxwell
  Federal aid to education...major federal aid programs for public schools primarily on the elementary and secondary levels. Tax Digest 43: 106-19, Fourth Quarter 1965   *475

Burke, Arvid J.
  U.S. control of schools will grow. American School Board Journal 153: 26-27, November 1966   476
          Concerning a shift of control over education from the states to the federal government with finance following the trend rather than preceding it.

California. Department of Education. Intradepartmental Committee on Federal Programs
  A guide to federal assistance programs for local educational agencies. 52p Sacramento, 1968   *477

California. Legislature. Joint Legislative Budget Committee.
  Office of the Legislative Analyst
  Federal aid programs in California; sixth report to the Legislature pursuant to the provisions of ACR 93 (1965). 136p (process) Sacramento, December 15, 1971   *478

California. Legislature. Senate. Fact Finding Committee on
   Education
   Proceedings of hearing: the interrelationship between state
   and federal education laws, November 30-December 1, 1965,
   San Francisco. 189p (process) Sacramento, 1965   *479
   ___, January 27, 1966, Los Angeles. 92p 1966

Center for Urban Education
   A history and description of ESEA Title I in New York City,
   1965-1968. 257p (mim) New York, June 1968   *480

Claremont Men's College. Institute for Studies in Federalism
   The impact of federal aid to primary and secondary education
   on selected southern California school districts; by John H.
   Baker. 51p Claremont, Calif., 1966   *481

Congressional Quarterly Service
   Federal role in education. ed. 2 66p Washington, D.C.,
   1967   *482
         Aid to education: major programs, 1945-65.

County allotments under Title I, Elementary and Secondary Education Act, for fiscal year 1968 based upon $1.2 billion ap-
   propriation distributed under family income factors of
   $2,000 and $3,000 with county savings clause added. Congressional Record, December 1, 1967: 34525-653   483

Drinan, Robert F.
   Reflections on the implications of Title I of the Elementary
   and Secondary Education Act of 1965. Catholic Lawyer 15:
   179-88, Summer 1969   484

Freeman, Roger A.
   Federal aid to schools 1965 model; before U.S. Senate Com-
   mittee on Labor and Public Welfare, February 4, 1965. Tax
   Digest 43: 9-11+, First Quarter 1965   *485

Guthrie, James W.
   The distribution of federal school aid funds: who wins?
   Educational Administration Quarterly (University Council for
   Educational Administration) 6: 47-61, Winter 1970   486

Keating, Barbara E.
   Federal aid to education: support or control? Educational
   Perspectives (University of Hawaii, College of Education) 9:
   18-23, October 1970   487

Munger, Frank J.
   The politics of federal aid to education; before American
   Political Science Association, 1965 annual meeting. 13p
   (process) 1965   *488

New York State. University of the State of New York. State
   Education Department. Bureau of Educational Finance Research
   Federal aid paid to New York school districts; a report and
   analysis, 1967-68 and 1968-69. 129p (mim) Albany, 1971
                                                            489

New York State. University of the State of New York. State
   Education Department. Division of Educational Finance
   Cooperative federalism: the federal role in the support of
   education in an urban society; by Richard C. Schilling. 57p
   (process) Albany, June 1969   *490

Osman, Jack W.
   The dual impact of federal aid on state and local government
   expenditures. National Tax Journal 19: 362-72, December
   1966   *491

Reed, Wayne O.
   Federal-state cooperation for education. Popular Government
   (University of North Carolina, Institute of Government) 32:
   1-5, May 1966   *492

Rowland, Howard S. and Wing, Richard L.
   Federal aid for schools, 1967-1968 guide; the complete handbook for the local school district. 396p New York, Macmillan, 1970   493

The schools cry for more federal aid: faulty tax bases and re-
   luctant voters are fast making it impossible to meet rising
   costs. Business Week, October 9, 1971: 56-58   494

Southern Center for Studies in Public Policy. Washington Research Project and NAACP Legal Defense and Educational Fund,
   Inc.
   Title I of ESEA: is it helping poor children? a report. ed.2
   73p Washington, D.C., December 1969   *495
          C. 3: Title I in place of state and
          local money.

Syracuse University Research Corporation. Policy Institute
   Federal aid to public education: who benefits? by Joel S.
   Berke and others. 84p (mim) Syracuse, January 31, 1971
          Study of five state sample (California,   *496
          New York, Michigan, Massachusetts, Texas).
   Same title: 83p (92:1, Com.Print) U.S. Senate Select Com-
   mittee on Equal Educational Opportunity, April 1971

Tax Institute of America
   Federal-state-local fiscal relationships; symposium, November 29-December 1, 1967. 502p Princeton, N.J., 1968   *497
          Federal-state-local responsibility in

education, by Robert C. Brown, p. 216-22;
Relative federal, state and local responsibility in education, by Lynn A. Stiles
and Lorne H. Woollatt, p. 223-48.

Tiedt, Sidney W.
The role of the federal government in education.   243p   New
York, Oxford University Press, 1966   498
Bibliography, p. 230-35.

U.S. Congress. House
H.R. 12695, the quality school assistance act of 1972; statement. Congressional Record, January 27, 1972: H392-93   499

U.S. Congress. House. Representative Alphonzo Bell and Others
The crisis in urban education. Congressional Record, September 26, 1968: 28435-81   500

U.S. Congress. House. Representative John G. Dow
Legislation to ease local property tax burden for local educational costs. Congressional Record, March 23, 1971: H1917
-20   *501
Reprinted: U.S. Senate Select Committee on Equal Educational
Opportunity, Equal educational opportunity--1971, hearings,
pt. 16D-3, p. 8579-85

U.S. Congress. House. Committee on Education and Labor
Education goals for 1965.   170p   (89:1, Com. Print) Washington D.C., January 1965   502

Elementary and secondary education amendments of 1966; report to accompany H.R. 13161.   134p   (89:2, H.Rep. no. 1814)
Washington, D.C., 1966   503

Elementary and secondary education amendments of 1967; hearings on H.R. 6230, March 2-20, 1967. 2pts (90:1) Washington, D.C., 1967   504

Elementary and secondary education amendments of 1967; report to accompany H.R. 7819.   100p   (90:1, H.Rep. no. 188)
Washington, D.C., 1967   505

Oversight hearings on elementary and secondary education
programs; hearings on H.R. 17861, May 13-July 15, 1970.
993p (91:2) Washington, D.C., 1971   506

School assistance in federally affected areas: a study of
Public Laws 81-874 and 81-815; final report, December 1969,

to Office of Education; by Harold A. Hovey and others, Battelle Memorial Institute.   214p   (91:2, Com.Print) Washington, D.C., 1970   *507

U.S. Congress. House. Committee on Education and Labor. General Subcommittee on Education
Impact aid reform act of 1970; hearings on H.R. 16307 and H.R. 16384, March 23-April 22, 1970. 600p (91:2) Washington, D.C., 1970   508

[Hearings on financing elementary and secondary education, February 28-March 1, 1972.] Congressional Quarterly, March 11, 1972: 559-70   *509

U.S. Congress. House. Republican Task Force on Education
Materials on financing schools. Congressional Record, January 18, 1972: E1-28   510

U.S. Congress. Senate
S. 3165, the educational quality act of 1972; text; statement. Congressional Record, February 14, 1972: S1586-87
                                                                 511

S. 3322, to encourage state and local governments to decrease their reliance on real property taxes as the principal means of funding expenditures for education; text; statement. Congressional Record, March 9, 1972: S3703-06   512

S. 3779, elementary and secondary education assistance act of 1972; text; statement. Congressional Record, June 29, 1972: S10606-16   513

U.S. Congress. Senate. Committee on Government Operations. Subcommittee on Intergovernmental Relations
Bibliography of federal grants-in-aid to state and local governments, 1964-1969; by Legislative Reference Service, pursuant to S.Res. 310, 91st Cong. 456p (process) (91:2, Com.Print)   Washington, D.C., October 2, 1970   *514

[Hearings on property tax reform, May 4, 9, 1972.] Congressional Record, May 4, 1972: S7251-53; Congressional Quarterly, May 20, 1972: 1152   *515

U.S. Congress. Senate. Committee on Labor and Public Welfare
Elementary and secondary education amendments of 1966; report to accompany S. 3046. 155p (89:2, S.Rep. no. 1674) Washington, D.C., 1966   516

Elementary and secondary education act amendments of 1967; report to accompany H.R. 7819. 190p (90:1, S.Rep. no. 726) Washington, D.C., November 6, 1967   517

U.S. Congress. Senate. Committee on Labor and Public Welfare.
Subcommittee on Education
[Education revenue sharing act of 1971, S. 1669; hearings,
October 27-28, November 3, 1971.] Congressional Quarterly,
November 13, 1971: 2358-59   *518

Elementary and secondary education act amendments of 1967
with background materials and tables. 210p (90:2, Com.
Print) Washington, D.C., 1968   519

Elementary and secondary education act of 1965; hearings on
S. 370, January 26-February 11, 1965. 6v (89:1) Washington, D.C,, 1965   *520

Notes and working papers concerning the administration of
programs authorized under Title I of Public Law 89-10, the
Elementary and Secondary Education Act of 1965 as amended by
Public Law 89-750. 2pts (90:1, Com.Print) Washington,
D.C., May 1967   *521

Statistical tables showing Pub.L. 874 and Pub.L. 89-10 en-
titlement by impacted area school districts. 115p (89:2,
Com.Print) Washington, D.C., June 1966   *522

U.S. Congress. Senate. Select Committee on Equal Educational
Opportunity
Equal educational opportunity; hearings, April 20, 1970-
November 30, 1971. 21pts (91:1-2) Washington, D.C., 1970-
71   *523
          Pt. 7: Inequality of economic resources;
          Pt. 16A-D (1-3): Inequality in school
          finance.

U.S. Department of Health, Education and Welfare
Report of the Commissioner's Ad Hoc Group on School Finance.
Reprinted: U.S. Senate Select Committee on Equal Educational
Opportunity, Equal educational opportunity--1971, hearings,
pt. 16D-3, p. 8355-412   *524

U.S. Department of Health, Education and Welfare. Office of
Education
The first year of Title 1, Elementary and Secondary Educa-
tion Act of 1965. 109p+ (mim) Washington, D.C., 1965   525

Title I/Year II; the second annual report of Title I of the
Elementary and Secondary Education Act of 1965, School Year
1966-67. 131p Washington, D.C., 1968   526

U.S. Department of Health, Education and Welfare. Secretary
Memorandum for the President, summarizing recent developments
in the field served by HEW, January 25, 1968. Weekly Comp-

ilation of Presidential Documents, January 29, 1968: 125-26
    Includes: Activities under Title I of   *527
    Elementary and Secondary Education Act.

U.S. Department of Health, Education and Welfare. Urban Educ-
ation Task Force
Final report, January 5, 1970.   528
Reprinted: Congressional Record, January 19, 1970: H9-15,
January 20, 1970: E21-77
Same: The Urban Education Task Force report, by Wilson C.
Riles. 369p New York, Praeger Publishers, 1970

U.S. Department of the Treasury. Division of Government Finan-
cial Operations
Federal aid to states, fiscal year 1971. 20p Washington,
D.C., 1972?   *529

U.S. Library of Congress. Legislative Reference Service
Federal educational policies, programs and proposals: a sur-
vey and handbook; by Charles A. Quattlebaum. 2pts (90:2,
H.Doc. no. 398) Washington, D.C., December 1968   *530

U.S. President
The budget message, 1972. Congressional Record, January 24,
1972: H179-87   531
        "Schools need emergency assistance now to
        make necessary adjustments to provide equal
        education opportunity."

Elementary and Secondary Education Amendments of 1967 (Pub.
L. 90-247); statement on signing, January 2, 1968. Weekly
Compilation of Presidential Documents, January 8, 1968: 29-
31   *532

Educational reform; message to the Congress, March 3, 1970.
Weekly Compilation of Presidential Documents, March 9, 1970:
304-14   *533

Special revenue sharing for education; message to the Con-
gress, April 6, 1971. Weekly Compilation of Presidential
Documents, April 12, 1971: 598-602   *534
Same: Congressional Record, April 6, 1971: H2469-71
Same: Congressional Quarterly, April 9, 1971: 826-28
Comment: Another look at education revenue sharing, by Char-
les B. Saunders, Jr. Congressional Record, October 19, 1971:
S16496-98

The state of the union; message to the Congress, January 20,
1972. (92:2, H.Doc. no. 201) Congressional Record, January 20, 1972: H145-60   535
        Includes: Financing our schools.

Washington University. Institute for Urban and Regional Studies
The Elementary and Secondary Education Act: a distributional
analysis; by David Barkin and Walter Hettich.   30p   (mim)
(Working paper EDA 8)   St. Louis, April 1968   *536

Weidenbaum, Murray L. and Swenson, Norman P.
Federal aid to education and low-income areas. Educational
Administration Quarterly 2: 225-33, Autumn 1966   537

Willingham, Ed
Nixon administration seeks massive change in federal school
-aid procedures. National Journal (Center for Political Research, Washington, D.C.) 3: 323-32, February 13, 1971   538

PROGRAMS AND PROPOSALS FOR
FINANCING LOCAL PUBLIC SCHOOLS

Performance Contracting

Under performance contracting, private industry--producers of teaching materials and electronic or computerized instruction machinery--go into the schools and, in return for a fee, attempt to raise the level of student achievement, particularly among the disadvantaged. If a contracting company fails to produce the level agreed upon with a local school board, it refunds part of the fee.

In March 1969, three school districts in Texarkana (Texas and Arkansas) were awarded a planning grant by the U.S. Office of Education under the Dropout Prevention Amendment (Title 8 of the Elementary and Secondary Education Act). The Texarkana School District contracted with the Institute for Politics and Planning for management support and program planning assistance. The U.S. Office of Economic Opportunity launched a major performance contracting project costing between $3.5 and $5.5 million and involving 12,000 to 34,000 students. When school began in September 1970, 24 different districts were selected for implementation of the approaches of six different companies.

Materials relating to performance contracting include the following:

Almost everything you need to know about performance contracting. American School Board Journal 159: 28-35, October 1971
539

Berson, Minnie P.
Back to Gary. Childhood Education 48: 51-55, October 1971
540

Texarkana and Gary: a tale of two performance contracts. Childhood Education 47: 339-40, March 1971 *541
Reprinted: U.S. Senate Select Committee on Equal Educational Opportunity, Equal educational opportunity--1971; hearings, pt. 16D-1, p. 7780-84

Bess, Donovan
Banneker School a success; a bold experiment [in Gary, Ind. school, carried out by Behavioral Research Laboratories, Palo Alto.] San Francisco, Chronicle, March 22, 1976: 6 542

68

Blaschke, Charles
   From gold stars to green stamps; the first year in performance contracting. Nation's Schools 88: 51-55, September
   1971   543

   Performance contracting. Nation's Schools 89: 37+, March
   1972   544

   Performance contracting costs, management reform and John Q.
   Citizen. Phi Delta Kappan 53: 245-47, December 1971   545
      Includes: Cost comparisons of experimental
      performance contracts in elementary reading
      (12 control programs, 10 experimental pro-
      grams).

Borick, Gary D., ed.
   Accountability: a symposium. Journal of Research and Development in Education 5: 1-96, Fall 1971   546
      A historical note on accountability in
      education, by Leon M. Lessinger;
      Motivation and performance contracting,
      by Brian Frieden;
      Accountability through performance con-
      tracting in Wichita, by Samuel Spaght.

Boutwell, William D.
   What is "performance contracting" as applied to schools?
   PTA Magazine 65: 21-23, October 1970   547

Campbell, Robert E.
   Accountability and Stone Soup. Phi Delta Kappan 53: 176-78,
   November 1971   548

Cass, James
   Profit and loss in education. Saturday Review, August 15,
   1970: 39-40   549
      Concerning Texarkana contract with Dorsett
      Educational System to take over schools.

Contracts: negative verdict on a teaching program. New York
   Times, February 6, 1972: 9E   560
      Concerning O.E.O's experiment.

The customers pass the test--or else. Business Week, September 12, 1970: 42+   561

Death knell of performance contracting? Educational Product
   Report 4: 2, May 1971   562

Educators OK industry in ghetto schools. Nation's Schools 85:
   108, March 1970   563

Elam, Stanley
  The age of accountability dawns in Texarkana. Phi Delta
  Kappan 51: 509-14, June 1970   564

An "F" for most performance contracting; the results aren't
all in yet, but the OEO is flunking industry's stab at teaching. Business Week, March 25, 1972: 84-85   565

Farr, Roger and Others
  How to make a pile in performance contracting. Phi Delta
  Kappan 53: 367-69, February 1972   566

Filogamo, Martin J.
  New angle on accountability: performance contract program
  in the Texarkana schools. Today's Education 59: 53, May
  1970   567

Finley, Grace J.
  Reforming public education [businessmen's attitudes toward
  performance contracting, etc.]. Conference Board Record 9:
  29-33, January 1972   568

Free enterprise for schools. Time Magazine, August 24, 1970:
  58+   569

Freeman, Roger
  The concept of accountability in education. University
  Bookman 11: 77, Summer 1971   570
  Reprinted: Congressional Record, September 15, 1971: E9590-
  93

Gary's novel school-score after a year. U.S. News and World
  Report, October 25, 1971: 61   *571
        Gary, Ind. contract with Behavioral Research
        Laboratories to restructure the teaching
        system at Banneker Elementary School.

Gehret, Kenneth
  Performance contracting: how does it score? Christian Science Monitor, January 3, 1972: 2d sec. p. 7   572

Gillis, James C., Jr.
  Performance contracting for public schools. Educational
  Technology 9: 17-20, May 1969   573

Harrison, Charles H.
  Who is accountable? private industry; teachers. Scholastic
  Teacher, Junior/Senior High, November 2, 1970: 12-13+   574

Hottleman, Girard D.
Performance contracting is a hoax! Education Digest 37: 1-
4, September 1971   575

Janssen, Peter
OEO as innovator: no more rabbits out of hats. Saturday
Review, February 5, 1972: 40-43   576

Kaufman, Bel
Will this boy's curriculum manager deserve an apple this
year [Gary, Ind., Banneker School]. Today's Health 49: 20-
23, September 1971   577

King, Seth S.
Pupils improve in school run by private company. New York
Times, September 29, 1971: 1+   578
        Concerning Gary, Ind. Schools Superintendent
        report on first year of four-year experimental
        program.

Lessinger, Leon M.
Accountability in public education: performance contracts;
before Conference on Testing Problems, Education Testing
Service, New York City, November 1969. Today's Education
59: 52-53, May 1970   579

Martin, Reed
Performance contracting: making it legal. Nation's Schools
87: 62-64, January 1971   580

Mecklenburger, James A.
Performance contracting report. Educational Technology 11:
6, May; 4, July; 62, September; 6, October; 16, November
1971   581

Performance contracts? one view. Educational Leadership 29:
297-300, January 1972   582

Mecklenburger, James A. and Wilson, John
Behind the scores at Gary [Banneker Contracted Curriculum
Center]. Nation's Schools 88: 28-29, December 1971   583

Learning C.O.D.: can the schools buy success [in Gary, Ind.]
Saturday Review, September 18, 1971: 62-65+   584

The performance contract in Gary. Phi Delta Kappan 52: 406-
10, March 1971   585

Performance contracting in Cherry Creek? Phi Delta Kappan
53: 51-54, September 1971   586

Michigan. Department of Education
  Introduction to guaranteed performance contracting. 51p
  Lansing, March 1971   587

Money-back schools: unclear balance sheets. Time, October 11,
  1971: 78   588

Moscove, Francine
  The experiment at Banneker School. (Writers workshop pam-
  phlet no. 3) May 1971   589
  Reprinted: U.S. Senate Select Committee on Equal Educational
  Opportunity, Equal educational opportunity--1971; hearings,
  pt. 16D-1, p. 7757-78

Murphy, Betty
  Performance contracting: where teaching and technology meet.
  Opportunity (U.S. Office of Economic Opportunity), August-
  September 1971: 2-9   590

National Committee for Support of the Public Schools
  Performance contracting: a road to accountability? by Marian
  F. Bendixsen. 8p (Special report) Washington, D.C.,
  March 1971   *591
            Table: Where guaranteed performance con-
            tracting is happening.

National Education Association. Research Division
  Accountability, vouchers and performance contracting; teacher opinion poll. Today's Education 60: 13, December 1971
                                                         592

National School Boards Association
  Performance contracting: a guide for school board members
  and community leaders; edited by William E. Dickinson. 72p
  Evanston, Ill., 1971   593

A novel plan for teaching gets low grades in new report [tests
  by U.S. Office of Economic Opportunity in 77 school districts in 18 cities]. U.S. News and World Report, February
  14, 1972: 52   *594

Oregon.University. ERIC Clearinghouse on Educational Management
  Accountability and performance contracting. 10p Eugene,
  1971?   595

Performance contracting; editorial. Nation's Schools 87: 7,
  March 1971   596

Performance contracting; an experiment. National Education
Association, Research Bulletin 49: 123-25, December 1971
<u>597</u>

Performance contracting as catalyst for reform [in Texarkana].
Educational Technology 9: 5-9, August 1969   <u>598</u>

Porter, Otha L.
Contracted school: instrument of educational change. Journal of Negro Education 40: 233-39, Summer 1971   <u>599</u>

Private firms in the public schools--one year of performance
contracting. Education Turnkey News (Educational Turnkey
Systems, Inc., Washington, D.C.), February-March 1971   <u>600</u>

Rand Corporation
Accountability, program budgeting and the California educa-
tional information system; a discussion and a proposal; by
J.A. Farquhar. 36p (R-637-CC/RC) Santa Monica, April
1971   <u>601</u>
Abstract: Selected Rand Abstracts 9 (4): 37, 1971

Case studies in educational performance contracting; pre-
pared for the U.S. Department of Health, Education and Wel-
fare. 6v (R-900/1-6) Santa Monica, December 1971   <u>602</u>
V. 1: Conclusions and implications, by
Polly Carpenter and George R. Hall;
V. 2: Norfolk, Virginia, by P. Carpenter;
V. 3: Texarkana, Arkansas, Liberty-Eylau,
Texas, by P. Carpenter and others;
V. 4: Gary, Indiana, by G. R. Hall and
M.L. Rapp;
V. 5: Gilroy, California, by M. L. Rapp;
V. 6: Grand Rapids, Michigan, by G. C.
Sumner.

Performance contracting in education and the Rand/HEW study;
by G. R. Hall. 13p (P-4682) Santa Monica, July 1971   <u>603</u>
Abstract: Selected Rand Abstracts 9 (4): 68, 1971

Performance contracting in education: an introductory over-
view; by G. R. Hall and J. P. Stucker. 26p (P-4659) Santa
Monica, July 1971   <u>604</u>
Abstract: Selected Rand Abstracts 9 (4): 66, 1971

The Rand/HEW study of performance contracting in education;
by G. R. Hall and J. P. Stucker. 11p (P-4558) Santa Monica, January 1971   <u>605</u>
Abstract: Selected Rand Abstracts 9 (4): 58, 1971

Rand Corporation
The performance contracting concept; by J. P. Stucker and
G. R. Hall. 83p (R-699/1-HEW) Santa Monica, May 1971   606
Abstract: Selected Rand Abstracts 9 (4): 41, 1971

The performance contracting concept; appendix: a critique of
the theory; by J. P. Stucker. 56p (R-699/2-HEW) Santa
Monica, May 1971   607
Abstract: Selected Rand Abstracts 9 (4): 41, 1971

Reading, writing and profit [for Dorsett Education Systems of
Norman, Okla.]. Business Week, October 4, 1969: 104   608

Reynolds, Jerry D.
Performance contracting; proceed with caution. English
Journal 60: 102-06+, January 1971   609
Same title: Education Digest 36: 5-7, April 1971

Rosenthal, Jack
Performance contracts lose luster. New York Times, January
10, 1972: 25E   610
        Concerning Rand Corporation evaluation of
        five contracts.

Saretsky, Gary
Every kid a hustler. Phi Delta Kappan 52: 595-96, June 1971
                                                       611

Schiller, Jeffry
Performance contracting; some questions and answers. American Education 7: 3-5, May 1971   612

Schwartz, Ronald
Accountability--special editorial report. Nation's Schools
85: 31-33, June 1970   613

Performance contracts: what industry thinks. Nation's
Schools 86: 53-55, September 1970   614

Star, Jack
We'll educate your kids or your money back. Look 35: 56+,
June 15, 1971   615

U.S. Congress. Senate. Senator W. E. Brock
Education: small returns on a big investment [performance
contracting, voucher system]. Congressional Record, April
27, 1972: S6721-23   616

Where private firm runs public schools [in Gary, Ind.]. U.S.
News and World Report, October 12, 1970: 41   *617

Where the action is: Dallas contracting. Nation's Schools
88: 46-47, December 1971   <u>618</u>

Will industry run our ghetto schools? Nation's Schools 85:
37+, January 1970   <u>619</u>

Willingham, Ed
  Performance contracting in schools tests administrations'
  "accountability" idea. National Journal (Center for Political Research, Washington, D.C.) 2: 2324-32, October 24,
  1970   <u>620</u>

Wilson, John
  Performance contracting: an experiment in accountability
  [in Texarkana]. Instructor 80: 21-22, June-July 1971   <u>621</u>

Voucher System

A voucher is "a convenient label for certification which the
government would issue to parents, parents would give to an
eligible school, and the school would return to the government for cash."

      Center for the Study of Public Policy
        Education vouchers; a report on financing ele-
        mentary education by grants to parents. 348p
        (process) Cambridge, Mass., December 1970   <u>*622</u>
          Appendix C: Constitutional problems;
          Appendix D: Model voucher demonstration
          statute;
          Appendix F: Treatment of Title I funds
          in a demonstration.

In Alum Rock Union Elementary School District in San Jose, California, a voucher experiment will begin in Fall 1972. The
two-year "transitional" program of the U.S. Office of Economic
Opportunity will provide parents of 4,000 children with vouchers to be used as a form of tuition in enrolling their children in a choice of educational programs to be offered in six
Alum Rock public schools. The basic vouchers will be worth
about $680 a year for children through the sixth grade and
$970 for seventh and eighth grades--the present state and lo-
cal per student expenditure (San Francisco Chronicle, April
25, 1972: 2).

      Levin, Joel M.
        The Alum Rock experiment; parents "buy" their
        child's education. San Francisco Sunday Exam-
        iner and Chronicle, This World, May 21, 1972:
        18   <u>623</u>

Voucher experiment begins at Alum Rock. California Journal 3: 148, May 1972   *624

Materials relating to a voucher plan for financing education
include the following:

Allen, James E., Jr.
USOE: plans, priorities for the 70's; interview. Nation's
Schools 85: 49-53, May 1970   625

American Conservative Union
The voucher system; by Yale Brozen and Roman L. Weil.   626
Reprinted: Congressional Record, May 6, 1971: S6355-59

Areen, Judith
Education vouchers. Harvard Civil Rights--Civil Liberties
Law Review 6: 466-504, May 1971   *627

Beckler, John
Voucher plan faces scrutiny of Congress [House Committee on
Education and Labor]. School Management 15: 6+, June 1971
       628

Berube, Maurice R.
The trouble with vouchers. Community (New York City University, Queens College, Institute for Community Studies)
3: 1-2+, November 1970   *629
Same title: Commonweal 93: 414-17, January 29, 1971

Boutwell, William D.
The voucher system? PTA Magazine 65: 12, February 1971   630

Branan, Karen
Vouchers: schools in the market place. Scholastic Teacher,
Junior/Senior High, January 11, 1971: 6-8   631

California. Legislature. Assembly. Committee on Education
Interim hearing on voucher system for education, San Jose,
October 23, 1970. 18p (process) Sacramento, 1970   *632

California. Legislature. Senate. Committee on Education
Voucher systems and contractor proposals; proceedings of
hearings, January 12-13, 1971. 296p (process) Sacramento,
1971   *633
       Includes: A model statute designed for
       adoption by a state, and particularly
       adapted to the state of California.

California Taxpayers' Association
Transcript of 45th annual meeting and fourth tax seminar,

February 23-24, 1971, Beverly Hills. 100p (process) Sacramento, 1971   *634
          Strengthening public education through
          accountability, by Wilson Riles;
          Vouchers and the entrepreneur, by Allen
          Calvin;
          State views against vouchers, by Neil
          Sullivan;
          Federal concern with vouchers, by David
          Boesel;
          Vouchers and minorities, by David San-
          chez;
          Legislative outlook on vouchers, by
          Leo Ryan.

Carr, Ray A. and Hayward, Gerald C.
     Education by chit: an examination of voucher proposals.
     Education and Urban Society 2: 179-91, February 1970   635

Coons, John E. and Sugarman, Stephen D.
     Family choice in education: a model state system for vouch-
     ers. California Law Review 59: 321-438, March 1971   *636
     Reprinted: 118p University of California, Berkeley, Insti-
     tute of Governmental Studies, 1971

Coyne, John R., Jr.
     The voucher system; why is it that educationists go red in
     the face when you mention the voucher system? National
     Review 23: 309-11, March 23, 1971   *637

Doyle, Denis P.
     Voucher experiments are proposed [in California]. Califor-
     nia Journal 2: 42-43, February 1971   *638

Education vouchers--challenge to the wall of separation? Val-
     paraiso University Law Review 5: 569-602, Spring 1971   639

Educational vouchers. Teachers College Record 72: 327-404,
     February 1971   640
          Education vouchers: a proposal for di-
          versity and choice, by Judith Areen and
          Christopher Jencks;
          Equity, option, and vouchers, by Stephen
          Arons;
          Vouchers--solution or sop? by David Sel-
          den;
          The economics of the voucher system, by
          Eli Ginsberg;
          Vouchers: a problem of scale, by Robert
          A. Dentler;

Voucher and the citizen, by Walter McCann
and Judith Areen.

Elford, George
The voucher plan debate. America 126: 87-91, January 29,
1972   641

Fleming, Barbara
The viability of voucher education. Appalachia 4: 29-38,
August-September 1971   *642

Glennan, Thomas
OEO experiments in education. Compact (Education Commission
of the States) 5: 3-5, February 1971   *643

Heller, Robert W.
Education vouchers: problems and issues. Educational Leadership 29: 424-29, February 1972   644

Janssen, Peter
Education vouchers. American Education 6: 9-11, December
1970   645

Jencks, Christopher
Giving parents money for schooling: education vouchers. Phi
Delta Kappan 52: 49-53, September 1970   646

Giving parents money to pay for schooling: education
vouchers. New Republic 163: 19-21, July 4, 1970   647

Is the public school obsolete? Public Interest (2): 18-27,
Winter 1966   *648

The Jencks' tuition voucher plan. America 122: 644-45, June
20, 1970   649

King, George
Educational vouchers. Illinois Education (Illinois Education Association) 60: 73, November 1971   650

King, Neil J.
Rebuilding the "fallen house"--state tuition grants for elementary and secondary education. Harvard Law Review 84:
1057-89, March 1971   651

Krughoff, Robert M.
Private schools for the public. Education and Urban Society
2: 54-79, November 1969   652

Lambert, Sam M.
[Voucher plan.] Today's Education 60: 64, May 1971   653
    Includes: National Education Association
    resolution (70-13) on voucher plan.

LaNoue, George R.
The politics of education [vouchers: the end of public education?] Teachers College Record 73: 304-19, December 1971
                                                        654

LaNoue, George R., ed.
Educational vouchers: concepts and controversies. 176p New
York, Teachers College Press, 1972   655

Lawrence, David
A constitutional way to avoid discrimination in aiding
schools. U.S. News and World Report, July 19, 1971: 88
                                                      *656

League of Women Voters of California
State education study kit, pt. 2. 37p+ (mim) San Francisco, October 1971   *657
    Includes: Federal plan for vouchers.

Lekachman, Robert
Vouchers & public education. New Leader 54: 9-14, July 12,
1971   658

Levin, Henry M.
The failure of the public schools and the free market rem-
edy. Urban Review (Center for Urban Education, New York
City) 2: 32-37, June 1968   *659

A "market economy" for the schools: OEO's new voucher system
.... Business Week, February 6, 1971: 76+   660

Marland, Sidney P.
New ideas for better schools; interview. U.S. News and
World Report, November 1, 1971: 80-85   *661

Massachusetts. General Court. Special Commission to Study Public Financial Aid to Nonpublic Primary and Secondary Schools
and Certain Related Matters
Nonpublic education in Massachusetts; report by Institute
for Educational Development, New York. 257p (process) Boston, May 1971   *662
    Voucher system, p. 108.

National Association of Secondary School Principals
Education and poverty revisited; by Thomas I. Ribich. Its
Bulletin 55: 17-25, April 1971   663

National Association of Secondary School Principals
  The voucher plan and performance contracting; by Walter Mc-
  Cann. Its Bulletin 55: 91-97, May 1971   664

No magic in vouchers. Nation 210: 773, June 29, 1970   665

Parents would buy schooling with a voucher. National Observer
  February 2, 1970: 1+   666

Reactions to vouchers: hostility, scepticism; school administrators opinion poll. Nation's Schools 87: 89, January
  1971   667

Ripon Society of Nashville
  Busing and its alternatives. Ripon Forum 8: 22-31, April
  1972   668
          Voucher system, p. 30-31.

Ryan, Leo
  Voucher system: a legislator's view. Black Politician 3:
  89-92, July 1971   *669

San Francisco, Calif. Board of Education
  [Study of voucher plan; by Abt Associates.] March 1972 670

Sizer, Theodore R. and Whitten, Phillip
  A proposal for a poor children's bill of rights. Psychology
  Today 2: 58-63, August 1968   671

A student-aid plan runs into a fight. U.S. News and World
  Report, August 9, 1971: 20-21   *672

Thackrey, Russell I.
  Case against the Wisconsin voucher plan. Current Issues in
  Higher Education 26: 121-28, 1971   673

U.S. Federal Reserve Bank of Philadelphia
  Capitalism in the classroom: education vouchers; by David
  W. Lyon. Its Business Review, December 1971: 3-10   *674

Use of public funds by private schools via educational vouchers: some constitutional problems. Pacific Law Journal 3:
  90+, January 1972   675

The voucher plan; NEA position. Today's Education 59: 80,
  November 1970   676

Wardle, F.
  Voucher system. National Elementary Principal 50: 84, May
  1971   677

West, E. G.
   Education and the state; a study in political economy.   ed.2
   243p   London, Institute of Economic Affairs, 1970   <u>678</u>
      Includes: voucher plan.

Willingham, Ed.
   OEO goes ahead with voucher plans despite opposition from
   teacher groups. National Journal (Center for Political Research, Washington, D.C.) 3: 939-46, May 1, 1971   <u>679</u>

Value-added Tax

The value-added tax (or VAT) is a general tax on sales of all
commodities and commercial services. It is imposed at each
stage of production from raw material to retail sales. Credit
is given at each stage for taxes already paid on business pur-
chases to prevent a compounding of taxes in the process of production.

      Smith, Dan T.
         ''VAT''--the most neutral tax. New York Times,
         February 28, 1972: 31C   <u>680</u>

In his state of the union address on January 20, 1972, the
President of the United States suggested that a national value-added tax could substitute for local property taxes as a
source for public school support.

      U.S. President
      The state of the union; address, January 20,
      1972. (92:2, H.Doc. no. 201) Washington,
      D.C., 1972   <u>681</u>
      Same: Congressional Record, January 20, 1972:
      H145-60

      School finance and intergovernmental relations;
      letter to the Chairman of the Advisory Commis-
      sion on Intergovernmental Relations [asking for
      a study of value-added tax], January 1972.
      Weekly Compilation of Presidential Documents,
      January 24, 1972: 92-93   <u>*682</u>

      Transcript of news conference on foreign and
      domestic matters, February 10, 1972. Weekly
      Compilation of Presidential Documents, Febru-
      ary 14, 1972: 413-19   <u>*683</u>
         The value-added tax one of several
         proposals considered by Treasury De-
         partment, Domestic Council and others
         as part of general tax reform.

U.S. Advisory Commission on Intergovernmental
Relations
[Eight special advisors for value-added tax
study]. 4p (process) (News release) Washington, D.C., February 5, 1972   684

ACIR survey shows public reaction to proposed
VAT, other taxes. 4p (Intergovernmental news
release) Washington, D.C., May 19, 1972   *685
Concerning poll conducted for Com-
mission by Opinion Research Corporation of Princeton, N.J.

ACIR spells out study plan on federal value-
added tax. MFOA Newsletter (Municipal Finance
Officers' Association of the United States and
Canada) 48: 24, March 1, 1972   686

Materials relating to the value-added tax include the following:

Aaron, Henry
The differential price effects of a value-added tax. National
Tax Journal 21: 162-75, June 1968   *687
Reprinted: (Reprint no. 150) Washington, D.C., Brookings
Institution, 1968

Another sales tax. New Republic, January 1, 1972: 13-14   688

Bartlett, Charles
Appeal of value-added tax grows.   689
Reprinted: Congressional Record, February 18, 1972: E1337

Beasley, Douglas
Value-added tax. Rossmoor News, February 23, 1972   690
Reprinted: Congressional Record, March 15, 1972: E2499

Bell, Don
The upcoming value-added tax bombshell; the red ink dilemma.
Don Bell Reports, January 28, 1972   691
Reprinted: Congressional Record, February 3, 1972: E758-60

Bogan, Eugene F.
A federal tax on value added--what's wrong with it? Plenty.
Taxes (Commerce Clearing House) 49: 600-08+, October 1971
                                                  692

Brookings Institution
Federal tax policy; by Joseph A. Pechman. 321p (Studies

of government finance) Washington, D.C., 1966   *693
    The value-added tax as a replacement for
    the corporation tax, p. 138-40.

Brookings Institution
    Setting national priorities: the 1973 budget. 468p   694
    Washington, D.C., 1972

California. University, Berkeley. Institute of Governmental
    Studies
    Agenda for local tax reform; by George F. Break, prepared
    for the California Advisory Commission on Tax Reform, Novem-
    ber 1968. 132p 1970   *695
        The value-added tax, p. 120-27.

California. University, Los Angeles. Institute of Government
    and Public Affairs
    VIT for VAT: is a valorem intangibles tax a democratic al-
    ternative for a value-added tax? by Donald G. Hagman. 29p+
    (mim) (MR-172) 1972   *696

Cantor, Arnold
    Tax justice: a giant step backward. AFL-CIO American Fed-
    erationist 79: 6-7, January 1972   *697

Chamber of Commerce of the United States
    The taxpayer's stake in tax reform; papers before conference
    on tax reform, February 14, 1968. 61p Washington, D.C.,
    1968   698
        A federal tax on value-added, by Arnold
        C. Harberger, p. 21-32.

Committee for Economic Development. Research and Policy Com-
    mittee
    A better balance in federal taxes on business; a statement
    on national policy. 37p New York, April 1966   *699
        C. 4: A value-added tax as part of the
        federal tax structure.

Coyne, Thomas J.
    The value-added tax. Business Review (University of Akron,
    Bureau of Business and Economic Research) 1: 10-17, Spring
    1970   *700
    Similar title: Atlanta Economic Review (Georgia State Uni-
    versity, Bureau of Business and Economic Research) 20: 38-
    40, July 1970

Due, John F.
    The value-added tax. Western Economic Journal 3: 165-71,
    Spring 1965   701

Due, John F.
Proposals for a federal value-added tax. Illinois Business
Review (University of Illinois, Bureau of Economic and Busi-
ness Research) 27: 6-8, February 1970   702

Ebel, Robert D. and Papke, James A.
A closer look at value-added tax: propositions and implications. National Tax Association, Proceedings, 1967: 155-71
                                                          703

Europe's value-added tax: model for U.S.? U.S. News and World
Report, March 6, 1972: 75-77   *704

First National City Bank of New York
Fiscal innovation: value-added tax. Its Monthly Economic
Letter, July 1968: 81-83   705

Forte, Francesco
On the feasibility of a truly general value-added tax: the
French experience. National Tax Journal 19: 337-61, Decem-
ber 1966   *706

Fowlkes, Frank V.
Economics Report/Administration leans to value-added tax to
help solve national fiscal crises. National Journal, February 5, 1972: 210-19   707

Harberger, Arnold C.
Let's try a value-added tax. Challenge (New York University) 15: 16-18+, November-December 1966   708

Harriss, C. Lowell
Value-added taxation; before annual tax conference of the
Public Finance Center, University of Pennsylvania, Fall 1969.
Wharton Quarterly (Wharton School of Finance and Commerce,
University of Pennsylvania) 4: 4-6+, Spring 1970   709

Heard, Niel
How the value-added tax can boost our economy. 32p New
York, Pilot Books, 1970   710

How value-added works in Europe; it is a prodigious source of
revenue there, but it can prove inflationary. Business
Week, February 26, 1972: 70   711

Indiana. Commission on State Tax and Financing Policy
Business taxation in Indiana; by Charles F. Bonser and
others. 353p Indianapolis, December 1966   *712
        Evaluation of tax on value-added and
        possible application in Indiana, p. 97-
        123.

Analysis of differential tax impact:
gross income, net income, value-added,
p. 124-34.

Indiana. University. School of Business. Division of Research
Projected compliance costs associated with the value-added
tax as proposed; by Phyllis A. Barker. Indiana Business
Review 47: 22-27, February-March 1972   713

Is there an important new tax in America's future? Finance
87: 40-43, December 1969   714

Lindholm, Richard W.
A plea for the value-added tax. Tax Review (Tax Foundation)
30: 17-24, May 1969   *715

Taxing retailing and service with value-added tax. Conference Board Record 9: 17-20, February 1972   716

The value-added tax: a short review of the literature. Journal of Economic Literature 8: 1178-89, December 1970   717
     Bibliography (100 items).
Comment: The value-added tax: critique of a review, by Mel
Krauss and Richard M. Bird. Journal of Economic Literature
9: 1167-73, December 1971

A value-added tax for the United States. Commercial and Financial Chronicle 207: 15+, February 15, 1968   718

Value-added tax vs. corporation income tax; before NABE annual meeting, September 1969. Business Economics (National
Association of Business Economists) 5: 62-65, January 1970
                                                               719

Value of value-added tax. AMS Professional Management Bulletin: Finance (Administrative Management Society) 10: 7-
11, February 1970   720

Matthíasson, Björn
What does it really mean?--the value-added tax. Finance and
Development 7: 40-46, March 1970   721
Reprinted: Congressional Record, April 4, 1972: S5294-96

Missorten, Walter
Some problems in implementing a tax on value-added. National
Tax Journal 21: 396-411, December 1968   *722

Morris, Alf
Value-added tax: a tax on the consumer. 23p (Fabian research series no. 284) London, Fabian Society, March 1970
                                                               723

National Governors' Conference
  Policy positions; adopted at 64th annual meeting, June 4-7,
  1972. 79p Lexington, Ky., 1972   *724
      National value-added tax, p. 26-27.

National Tax Association
  Proceedings, 1965. 782p Harrisburg, 1966   725
      Approach to introduction of value-added
      tax by federal government, by Richard
      W. Lindholm.

Oakland, William H.
  The theory of the value-added tax: a comparison of tax
  bases: incidence effects. National Tax Journal 20: 119-36,
  270-81, June, September 1971   *726
      Based largely upon doctoral thesis,
      "Theory of the value-added tax,"
      Massachusetts Institute of Technology,
      1964.

Papke, James A.
  Michigan's value-added tax after seven years. National Tax
  Journal 13: 350-63, December 1960   *727

Phillips, Lawrence C.
  Simplification of our tax structure and obtaining relief
  from balance of payments deficits: two possible benefits
  from the imposition of a value-added tax. Taxes (Commerce
  Clearing House) 49: 674-78, November 1971   728

Pogue, Thomas F. and Sgontz, L.G.
  Value-added vs. property taxation of business. Land Economics 47: 150-57, May 1971   *729

Quindry, Kenneth E. and Masten, John T., Jr.
  The pros and cons of state and local application of value-
  added tax. Tennessee Planner (Tennessee State Planning Commission) 31: 45-53, Winter 1972   *730

Semple, Robert B., Jr.
  President plans value-added tax to help schools; project
  would also cut local property taxes. New York Times, February 1, 1972: 1+   731

Shoup, Carl S.
  Consumption tax, and wages type and consumption type of
  value-added tax. National Tax Journal 21: 153-61, June 1968
                                                                *732

Silk, Leonard
   Is there a V.A.T. in your future? New York Times, February
   14, 1972: 29   733

   New kind of tax for the seventies--the VAT. San Francisco
   Sunday Examiner and Chronicle, Sunday Punch, February 20,
   1972: 2   734

   Value-added: guess who pays the tax. New York Times, February 6, 1972: 3E   735

Simonetti, Gilbert J.
   A value-added tax--is it coming to the U.S.? Tax Adviser
   (American Institute of Certified Public Accountants) 1: 135-
   37, February 1970   736

Smith, Dan Throop
   Value-added tax: the case for.   737
   Reprinted: Congressional Record, January 18, 1972: E19-22

Sullivan, Clara K.
   The tax on value-added. 340p New York, Columbia University
   Press, 1965   738
         Bibliography, p. 313-27.
         Appendix C: The Michigan business activities
         tax.

Surrey, Stanley S.
   A value-added tax for the United States--a negative view.
   Tax Executive 21: 151-72, April 1969   739
   Comment: The value-added tax--rebuttal of a negative view,
   by Richard W. Lindholm. Tax Executive 22: 85-92, January
   1970

Tax Foundation, Inc.
   Value-added taxes. 9p (mim) (Research bibliography no.
   45) New York, January 1971   *740

Tax Institute of America
   Alternatives to present federal taxes; symposium. 257p
   Princeton, N.J., 1964   *741
         Pt. 3: Alternatives to corporate income
         tax: value-added tax.

   Federal-state-local fiscal relationships; proceedings of a
   symposium, November 29-December 1, 1967. 502p Princeton,
   N.J., 1968   *742
         Value-added taxes, p. 132+.

Taxation With Representation
  The value-added tax; a preliminary analysis. v.p. Arling-
  ton, Va., 1972   743

Treasury mulls a different bite. Business Week, August 1,
  1970: 44   744

Two views: what about the value-added tax? by Jude Wanniski
  and Lindley H. Clark, Jr. Wall Street Journal, April 10,
  1972: 12   745

Ulmer, Melville J.
  How bad is VAT? If, ands, and buts of the value-added tax.
  New Republic, June 17, 1972: 15-17   746

U.S. Congress. House. Representative Joseph M. Gaydos
  [Telephone poll on value-added tax.] Congressional Record,
  June 28, 1972: E6558-59   747

U.S. Congress. House. Committee on Ways and Means
  Excise tax compendium; compendium of papers on excise tax
  structure, submitted in connection with the panel discussion on the same subject to be conducted on June 15-16, 1964.
  pt. 1 181p (88:2) Washington, D.C., 1964   *748
      Value-added taxation in relation to in-
      come, excise and sales taxation: the
      value-added tax, by Dan T. Smith;
      The economic effects of a federal
      value-added tax, by Earl R. Rolph,
      p. 89-107.

U.S. Congress. Joint Economic Committee
  [Hearings on proposals to replace local property taxes with
  a federal value-added tax as the method of financing public
  school systems, March 21-23, 1972.] Congressional Quarterly
  March 25, 1972: 685-86, April 1, 1972: 740-41; Congressional
  Record, March 22, 1972: S4505-09, March 28, 1972: S4936-43
                                                      *749

  The value-added tax; hearings, March 21-24, 1972. 221p (92:
  2) Washington, D.C., 1972   *750
      Appendix: Toward a new philosophy of taxa-
      tion, by Richard W. Lindholm;
      Statement of Communications Workers of
      America and American Federation of Teachers.

U.S. Congress. Joint Economic Committee. Subcommittee on International Exchange and Payments
  A review of balance of payments policies: hearings, January
  13-15, 1969. 257p (91:1) Washington, D.C., 1969   *751
      A value-added tax for the United States--

a negative view, by Stanley S. Surrey,
p. 50-60.

U.S. Congress. Senate. Senator James B. Pearson
The proposed value-added tax. Congressional Records, February 18, 1972: S2074   752
"A national sales tax is neither an equit-
able nor an effective means to alleviate
the financial crisis in schools."

U.S. Federal Reserve Bank of Philadelphia
A balance sheet for the value-added tax; by Edward G. Boehne.
Its Business Review, June 1969: 2-9   *753

[U.S.] Treasury mulls over VAT. Pacific Business Bulletin
(California Chamber of Commerce) 62:1, March 6, 1972   *754

A value-added tax making news. New York State Taxpayer (Citizens Public Expenditure Survey, Inc.) 33: 3, May-June 1972
                                                        *755

Value-added tax: possible relief for property owners. Congressional Quarterly, February 26, 1972: 440-42   *756

Aaron, Henry J. 115, 687
Abelson, Stuart, 4
Abt Associates, 670
Adams, John K., 5, 6
Alexander, C.K., 472
Alexander, Orville, 290
Alkin, Marvin C., 256
Allen, Dwight H., 163
Allen, James E., Jr., 152,
  174, 175, 625
Alum Rock Union Elementary
  School District, 623, 624
American Association of
  School Administrators, 116
American Conservative Union,
  626
American Council on Educa-
  tion, 117, 118
American Federation of Teach-
  ers, 750
American Political Science
  Association, 488
Anderson, J. W., 339
Anderson, Wendell R., 357
Andrews, Frederick, 48
Areen, Judith, 627, 640
Arizona-School financing, 60,
  224
Arkansas. Legislative Coun-
  cil, 225
Arnold, Max P., 288
Arons, Stephen, 640
Association of School Busi-
  ness Officials of the
  United States, 176

Baggett, Bryce, 391
Bailey, Stephen K., 474
Baker, John H., 481
Banovetz, James M., 293
Barker, Phyllis A., 713
Barkin, David, 374, 375, 536
Barlow, Robin, 119
Barr, Charles W., 127
Barr, W. Montfort, 159
Barro, S. M., 162
Bartlett, Charles, 689

Bateman, Worth, 7
Battelle Memorial Institute,
  418
Beam, David R., 293
Beasley, Douglas, 690
Beckler, John, 628
Behavioral Research Labora-
  tories, 542, 571
Bell, Alphonzo, 500
Bell, Don, 691
Bendixsen, Marian F., 85, 591
Bensfield, James A., 78
Benson, Charles S., 120, 177,
  202, 254
Bentley, Fred H., 407
Benton, E. Maxwell, 226, 227,
  475
Berke, Joel S., 121, 122, 393,
  496
Berson, Minnie P., 540, 541
Berube, Maurice R., 629
Bess, Donovan, 542
Billings, R. Bruce, 224
Bird, Richard M., 717
Blaschke, Charles, 152,
  543-45
Boehne, Edward G., 305, 753
Boesel, David, 634
Bogan, Eugene F., 692
Bonser, Charles F., 712
Borick, Gary D., 546
Boutwell, William D., 547,
  630
Boynton, Ralph E., 8
Branan, Karen, 631
Break, George F., 695
Brock, W. E., 616
Bronder, Leonard, 340
Brookings Institution, 693,
  694
Brown, Peter, 7
Brown, Robert C., 9, 497
Browning, R. Stephen, 143
Brownlee, O. H., 368, 369
Brozen, Yale, 626
Bruno, James E., 178, 179
Burke, Arvid J., 412, 476

California
  Advisory Commission on Tax
    Reform, 228, 229, 695
  Council on Intergovernmen-
    tal Relations, 230
  Department of Education
    Division of Public School
      Administration, 231,
      232
    Intradepartmental Commit-
      tee on Federal Programs,
      477
    State Board of Education,
      199, 201-03
    School Support Commit-
      tee, 233
    Statewide Council on
      Long-Range School Fi-
      nance Planning, 234
    State Committee on Public
      Education, 235
  Department of Finance. Tax
    Research Group, 236
  Federal aid programs, 477-
    79, 481
  Governor, 237, 242, 239
    See also Reagan, Ronald
  Governor's Commission on
    Educational Reform,
    238
  Judicial Council, 10
  Legislative-Executive Tax
    Study Group, 239
  Legislature
    Assembly
      Committee on Education,
        240, 632
      Committee on Revenue
        and Taxation, 241,
        242
      Interim Committee on Ed-
        ucation, 243
      Interim Committee on
        Revenue and Taxation,
        244
      Constitution Revision
        Commission, 245
      Joint Legislative Budget
        Committee. Office of
        the Legislative Analyst,
        246-51, 478

California
  Legislature
    Senate
      Committee on Education,
        11, 633
      Fact Finding Committee
        on Education, 248,
        252, 479
      Select Committee on
        School District Fi-
        nance, 11
    Property tax, 229, 230, 238,
      250, 252, 270
      See also Cases--Serrano
      v. Priest
    School finance, 1-45, 49,
      51, 55, 226-72, 601
    Supreme Court, 1-45
    University, Berkeley. In-
      stitute of Governmental
      Studies, 695
    University, Los Angeles.
      Institute of Government
      and Public Affairs, 255,
      256, 696
    Vouchers, 623, 624, 632,
      633, 638
California Chamber of Com-
  merce, 257
California Taxpayers' Assoc-
  iation, 634
Calvin, Allen, 634
Cameron, Peter C., 176
Campbell, Alan K., 68,
  123
Campbell, Robert E., 548
Cantor, Arnold, 697
Carpenter, Polly, 602
Carr, Ray A., 635
Carter, Robert L., 69
Cases, Court, 46, 59, 65, 75,
  98, 149
  Burrus v. Wilkerson, 46
  Hargrave v. Kirk, 46
  Hollins v. Shoftall, 60
  McGinnis v. Shapiro, 46
  MacInnes v. Ogilvie, 50
  Robinson v. Cahill, 57
  Rodriguez v. San Antonio
    Independent School Dis-
    trict, 54, 67

Cases, Court
  Serrano v. Priest, 1-45.
    67, 188, 310, 316, 416
  Spano v. Board of Education
    of Lakeland Central
    School, 58
  Sweetwater County Planning
    Committee v. Hinkle, 67
  Van Dusartz v. Hatfield,
    63, 67
Cass, James, 549
Cassidy, Joseph, 15
Catholic University. Center
  for National Policy Review,
  16
Center for Applied Research
  in Education, 124
Center for the Study of Pub-
  lic Policy, 622
Center for Urban Education,
  480
Chamber of Commerce of the
  United States, 698
Cherry Creek, 586
Chicago, Ill.-Schools, 289
Chicago. University. Center
  for Policy Study, 70
Childress, Jack R., 131
Citizens League of Minneap-
  olis and Hennepin County,
  358-60
Citizens Research Council of
  Michigan, 341-43
Claremont Men's College. In-
  stitute for Studies in
  Federalism, 481
Clark, Lindley H., Jr., 745
Cohen, David K., 50
Cohen, Edwin S., 160
Coleman, James S., 71, 74,
  93
Colman, William G., 180
Colorado
  Legislative Council, 273,
    274
  School financing, 273-75
Colorado Public Expenditure
  Council, 275
Committee for Economic Devel-
  opment, 71, 125, 699
Committee of Seventy, 440

Communications Workers of
  America, 750
Community-school financial
  relationships, 127
Conant, James B., 193
Conference on...
  Alternative Financing of
    Education, 122
  Economic Progress, 126
  State Financing of Public
    Schools, 173
  Testing Problems, 579
Conference to Review...Nation-
  al Education Finance Proj-
  ect, 399
Congress of Cities, 172
Congressional Quarterly, Inc.,
  473
Congressional Quarterly Serv-
  ice, 482
Connecticut
  Commission to Study...Met-
    ropolitan Government, 276
  General Assembly. Interim
    Committee on Education,
    277
  School financing, 277-80
  State Revenue Task Force,
    278
  University. Institute of
    Public Service, 279
Connecticut Public Expendi-
  ture Council, Inc., 280
Constitution and equal educa-
  tion opportunity, 70, 73,
  163
  See also U.S. Constitution
Coons, John E., 17, 18, 32,
  43, 182-84, 636
Cooper, Paul D., 160
Corporation income tax, 719,
  741
Council of Planning Librar-
  ians, 101, 127
Council of State Chambers of
  Commerce, 149
Council of the Great City
  Schools, 289
Cox, Ronald W., 259, 260
Coyne, John R., Jr., 637
Coyne, Thomas J., 700

Crawford, George J., 191
Cresap, McCormick and Paget,
Inc., 102
Culbertson, Jack, 128
Curran, William J., 20
Cuyahoga County, Ohio-School
districts, 419

Dahl, David S., 370
Daly, Charles U., 70
Daniere, Andre, 331
Davis, Otto A., 70
Dees, John W., 416
Dentler, Robert A., 640
Detroit, Mich.-Metropolitan
school finance, 340
Dickinson, William E., 593
Dimond, Paul R., 43
Dochterman, Clifford L., 52
Dorsett Educational System,
549, 608
Dow, John G., 501
Doyle, Denis P., 22, 638
Drinan, Robert F., 484
Due, John F., 701, 702
Dye, Thomas R., 185
Dyer, Henry S., 74
Dykes, Stephen E., 241

Ebel, Robert D., 703
Ecker-Racz, L. L., 186, 187
Education and Public Affairs,
107
Education Commission of the
States, 23, 52, 144, 188-97
Educational Research and De-
velopment Council of the
Twin Cities, 159
Educational Testing Service,
114, 579
Eisentrout, George M., 468
Elam, Stanley, 564
Elementary and Secondary Edu-
cation Act, 474, 480, 483,
484, 495, 521, 527, 536
Elford, George, 641

Falcon, James C., 114
Farber, M.A., 58
Farquhar, J.A., 601
Farr, Roger, 566

Federal assistance in finan-
cing local public schools,
140, 152, 473-538, 634
Federation of Tax Administra-
tors, 53
Filogamo, Martin J., 567
Financing of local public
schools, 100-72
Finley, Grace J., 568
First National City Bank of
New York, 705
Fleischman, Manly, 396
Fleming, Barbara, 642
Florida
Department of Education,
283
Legislature
House Appropriations Com-
mittee, 284
Legislative Intern Pro-
gram, 285
School financing, 46, 281-85
Flournoy, Houston I., 24
Forte, Francesco, 706
Fowlkes, Frank V., 707
Freeman, Roger, 485, 570
Frieden, Brian, 546
Fuller, Edgar, 442
Fund for Public Policy Re-
search, 160

Garber, Lee O., 117, 118
Garms, Walter I., 412
Garvue, Robert J., 130
Gary, Ind.-School contracts,
192, 540-42, 571, 577, 578,
583-85, 589, 602, 617
Gauerke, Warren E., 131
Gaydos, Joseph M., 747
Gehret, Kenneth, 572
George, W. Elmer, 286
George Washington University.
State-Local Finances Proj-
ect, 203
Georgia-Property tax, 286
Gillis, James C., Jr., 573
Gilroy, Calif.-Performance
contracting, 602
Ginsberg, Eli, 640
Gittell, Marilyn, 132
Glennan, Thomas, 192, 643

Goldstein, Stephen R., 25
Governmental Research Insti-
tute, Cleveland, 419, 420
Governmental Research Insti-
tute, Lincoln, 376
Graham, Robert L., 75
Grand Rapids, Mich.-Perfor-
mance contracting, 602
Grants-in-aid, Federal, 514
See also Federal assistance
in financing local public
schools
Grasberger, Friedrich J., 414
Great Plains Agricultural
Council, 167
Greater Toledo Municipal
League, 427-31
Greenbaum, William N., 39
Greene, Leroy, 262
Grieder, Calvin, 26, 133
Guthrie, James W., 76, 77,
134, 356, 486

Hack, Walter G., 135
Hady, Thomas F., 167
Hagman, Donald G., 696
Hall, George R., 192, 602-06
Hamilton, Lee, 27, 149
Harberger, Arnold C., 698,
708
Harper, Edwin H., 232
Harris, Laurence, 391
Harrison, Charles H., 574
Harrison, Forest W., 222
Harriss, C. Lowell, 709
Harvard Center for Law and
Education, 78
Hawaii
State financing of schools,
173, 287
University. Legislative Ref-
erence Bureau, 287
Hawkins, Joseph F., 58
Hayden, Francis G., 457
Hayward, Gerald C., 635
Heller, Robert W., 644
Herbers, John, 101
Hettich, Walter, 198, 536
Hey, Robert P., 136
Hickey, John K., 28
Hickrod, G. Alan, 79

Hillenbrand, Bernard F., 137
Hirsch, Werner Z., 255
Hogan, Lloyd L., 403
Horowitz, Harold W., 80, 81
Hottleman, Girard D., 575
Hovey, Harold A., 507
Howe, Harold, II, 138

Idaho
Legislature. Interim Tax
Study Committee, 288
Property tax, 288
Illinois
Constitution Research Group,
290
Governor, 291
Legislative Council, 292
Northern Illinois Univer-
sity. Center for Govern-
mental Studies, 293
School financing, 46, 289-
96
School Problems Commission,
294-96
Income tax for education, 414,
439
Indiana
Commission on State Tax and
Financing Policy, 297-99,
712
Legislative Council, 300,
301
School financing, 297-305
University
Bureau of Government Re-
search, 302
School of Business, 303-
05, 713
School of Education, 159
Inequality of educational op-
portunity, 1-99, 331
Institute for Chief State
School Officers, 142
International Association of
Assessing Officers, 29, 139
International Future Research
Conference, 255
Iowa
Governor's Conference on
Education, 306
School financing, 306-11

Iowa
  Taxation Study Committee,
    308
  University. Institute of
    Public Affairs, 309
Iverson, Evan, 438

James, H. Thomas, 128, 140
Janssen, Peter, 576, 645
Jarrett, James L., 71
Jencks, Christopher, 93, 152,
  192, 640, 646-49
Jesser, David L., 148
Johns, Roe L., 141, 148, 157,
  158
Johns, Thomas L., 169
Johnson, Ray H., 232
Johnson, Virgil K., 82
Jones, Howard R., 124
Jones, Thomas H., 111
Jordan, K. F., 196

Kansas
  Legislative Coordinating
    Council, 312
  Legislature
    Joint Committee...
      School Finance, 313
      State Tax Structure,
        314
      Special Committee on As-
        sessment and Taxation,
        315
  School financing, 312-16
Kaponen, Niilo, 276
Karsh, Norman, 101
Karst, Kenneth L., 30
Kaufman, Bel, 577
Keating, Barbara E., 487
Keiter, Robert B., 31, 46
Kelly, James A., 142,
  394
Kentucky
  Legislative Research Com-
    mission, 317-19
  School financing, 317-23,
    375
  University
    Center for the Study of
      State and Local Govern-
      ment Economics, 320

Kentucky
  University
    Office of Development
      Services and Business
      Research, 321
  Western Kentucky University,
    318
Keppel, Francis, 199
Keyserling, Leon H., 126
Kiesling, Herbert J., 297
Kindl, Kathryn L., 447
King, George, 650
King, Neil J., 651
King, Seth S., 578
Kirk, Russell, 83
Kirp, David, 43, 74, 93
Knoll, F. Jeannette, 302
Kohler, Marie A., 283
Kolesar, John, 54
Kotin, Lawrence, 200
Krauss, Mel, 717
Kravitt, Jason H., 75
Krughoff, Robert M., 652
Kurland, Philip B., 70

Lambert, Sam M., 653
LaNoue, George R., 654, 655
Lausberg, Clem, 284, 285
Lawrence, David, 656
Lawyers' Committee for Civil
  Rights Under Law, 32, 143,
  144
League of Women Voters
  California, 263-65, 657
  Minnesota, 361
Legler, John, 374
Lekachman, Robert, 658
Lessinger, Leon M,, 125, 163,
  546, 579
Levin, Betsy, 271
Levin, Henry M., 125, 659
Levin, Joel M., 623
Leyton, Peter, 144
Liberty-Eylau, Tex.-Perfor-
  mance contracting, 602
Lile, Stephen E., 320
Lincoln, Neb.-Public schools,
  376
Lindholm, Richard W., 145,
  160, 432, 434, 715-20, 725,
  739, 750

Lindman, Erick L., 266
Lindsay, John V., 197
Lorette, Robert L., 412
Los Angeles Bureau of Munici-
  pal Research, 267, 268
Lutz, Harley L., 146
Lyon, David W., 445, 674

McAndrew, Gordon, 192
McCall, Tom, 435, 436
McCann, Walter, 640, 664
McKim, Bruce T., 228
McLoone, Eugene, 187, 222,
  410
McMahon, Patrick C., 288
McMurrin, Sterling M., 71,
  125
Maeroff, Gene I., 147
Maine
  Legislature. Legislative
    Research Committee, 324
  School financing, 324, 325
  University. Bureau of Pub-
    lic Administration, 325
Maine Property Tax Conference,
  325
Malis, Mrs. Louis A., 289
Marland, Sidney P., 661
Martin, Reed, 580
Maryland
  Commission to Study...Pub-
    lic Education, 326
  Legislative Council, 327
  School financing, 326-30
  Study Commission on the
    State Tax Structure, 328
Massachusetts
  Advisory Council on Educa-
    tion, 331, 332
  Department of Education,
    333, 334
  General Court
    Senate, 335
    Special Commission...
      Educational Facilities,
      336
    Financial Aid to Non-
      public Schools, 661
    Master Tax Plan, 337
  Legislative Research Coun-
    cil, 338

Massachusetts
  School financing, 331-38
Masten, John T., Jr., 730
Matthíasson, Björn, 721
Mecklenburger, James A., 581-
  86
Merriam, Robert E., 194
Metropolitan Council of the
  Twin Cities Area, 362, 363
Metropolitan fiscal dispari-
  ties, 210, 213
Michelman, Frank I., 84
Michigan
  Department of Education,
    344-46, 587
  Executive Office. Bureau of
    Programs and Budget, 346
  Governor, 339, 341, 342,
    346-49
  Governor's Commission on
    Educational Reform, 350
  Governor's Special Commis-
    sion on Land Use, 351
  Legislative Fiscal Agency,
    352
  Office of Planning Coordin-
    ation, 353
  School financing, 198, 339-
    56
  Value-added tax, 727,
    735
Milliken, William G., 346,
  354, 355
  See also Michigan. Governor
Milwaukee Metropolitan Area-
  School financing, 207
Minneapolis-St. Paul Metropol-
  itan Area, 370
Minnesota
  Governor, 364
  Governor's Advisory Commit-
    tee on Education, 365
  Governor's Property Tax
    Advisory Committee,
    366
  Legislature. Elementary and
    Secondary Education Com-
    mission, 367
  School financing, 47, 51,
    63, 357-70
  State Planning Agency, 368

Mississippi
 Department of Education, 371
 School financing, 371
Missorten, Walter, 722
Missouri
 School District Reorganiza-
  tion Commission, 372
 School financing, 372-75
Monroe County Educational
 Planning Committee, 414
Moore, Hullihen W., 460
Moretti, Bob, 261
Morgan, Daniel C., Jr., 457
Morphet, Edgar L., 141, 148
Morris, Alf, 723
Moscone, George, 257
Moscove, Francine, 589
Mosher, Edith K., 474
Munger, Frank J., 488
Murphy, Betty, 590
Myers, Phyllis, 33, 101

NAACP Legal Defense and Edu-
 cational Fund, Inc., 495
National Association of Busi-
 ness Economists, 719
National Association of Manu-
 facturers, 149
National Association of Sec-
 ondary School Principals,
 663, 664
National Clearinghouse for
 Legal Services, 150
National Committee for Sup-
 port of the Public Schools,
 85, 144, 151-53, 201,
 202, 591
National Conference on Gov-
 ernment, 208
National Education Associa-
 tion, 317, 653, 676
 Commission on Professional
  Rights..., 322
 Committee on Educational
  Finance, 154-56, 203,
  256
 Research Division, 592
National Education Finance
 Project, 157-59, 399
National Governors' Confer-
 ence, 724

National League of Cities,
 204
National Municipal League,
 208
National School Boards Assoc-
 iation, 435, 593
National Tax Association,
 160, 725
Nebraska
 Legislature, 378
 School financing, 376-79
 State Department of Educa-
  tion, 379
Neitring, Diana L., 81
Nevada
 Governor, 380
 Legislative Counsel Bureau,
  381
 School financing, 380, 381
New Hampshire
 General Court. Fiscal Com-
  mittee, 382
 State financing of schools,
  173, 382
New Jersey
 County and Municipal Govern-
  ment Study Commission,
  383
 Governor's Welfare Study
  Commission, 384
 Legislature. Senate and As-
  sembly Committees, 385
 School financing, 47, 49,
  56, 57, 60, 383-90
 State Aid to School Dis-
  tricts Study Commission,
  386, 387
 Superior Court, Hudson
  County, 57
 Tax Policy Committee, 388
New Jersey Taxpayers Associa-
 tion, 389
New Mexico
 Educational Research Com-
  mittee, 392
 School financing, 391,
  392
New York City, N.Y.
 ESEA, 480
 School financing, 393,
  394

New York State
  Commission on the Quality,
    Cost and Financing of...
    Education, 395, 404
  Department of Audit and
    Control, 397
  Federal aid, 489, 490
  School financing, 58, 60,
    197, 198, 393-415
  State Education Department,
    399, 400
    Bureau of Educational Fi-
      nance Research, 401-07,
      489
    Division of Educational
      Finance, 408, 490
    Information Center on Ed-
      ucation, 409
  Supreme Court. Westchester
    County, 58
  Temporary State Commission
    on the Constitutional Con-
    vention, 398
New York State Association of
  City Councils, 197
New York State Conference of
  Mayors and Other Municipal
  Officials, 35
New York State Educational
  Conference Board, 410
Newark, N.J. Office of Eco-
  nomic Development, 390
Norfolk, Va.-Performance con-
  tracting, 602
North Carolina
  Governor's Study Commission
    on the Public School Sys-
    tem, 417
  School financing, 416, 417
Northern Illinois University.
  Center for Governmental
  Studies, 293
Norton, John K., 126
Nyquist, Ewald B., 399, 400

Oakland, William H., 726
Ogilvie, Richard B., 291
Ohio
  General Assembly. House.
    Bipartisan Select Commit-
    tee on Tax Revision, 421

Ohio
  Legislative Service Commis-
    sion, 422, 423
  School financing, 418-23
Ohio State University Re-
  search Foundation, 108
Opinion Research Corporation,
  Princeton, N.J., 685
Oregon
  Department of Education,
    433
  Governor, 434-36
  Governor's Education Im-
    provement Advisory Commis-
    sion, 433, 437
  School financing, 432-39
  University
    Bureau of Governmental
      Research and Service,
      438
    ERIC Clearinghouse on
      Educational Management,
      595
    School Study Council, 439
Osman, Jack W., 491
PACE, 424, 425
Papke, James A., 703, 727
Pauly, Mark V., 161
Paus, Gregory S., 439
Pearson, James B., 752
Pechman, Joseph A., 693
Peck, John E., 205, 206, 298,
  303
Pennsylvania
  Board of Education, 441,
    442
  School financing, 440-47
Performance contracts, 101,
  112, 152, 194, 467, 539-621
Phelps, James, 355
Philadelphia, Pa.-Financial
  crisis, 440, 445
Phillips, Lawrence C., 728
Pierce, Wendell H., 192
Pleeter, Saul, 304
Pogue, Thomas F., 729
Polley, John W., 412
Porter, Otha L., 599
Pratt Institute, 413
Program for Action by Citi-
  zens in Education, 424, 425

Property taxes, 4-45, 53, 54, 65, 89, 138, 145, 170, 178, 181, 225, 501, 512, 681, 749
  California, 229, 230, 238, 244, 248, 250, 252, 253, 270
  Colorado, 275
  Florida, 282
  Georgia, 286
  Idaho, 288
  Iowa, 311
  Massachusetts, 335
  Michigan, 339, 340, 350
  Minnesota, 366, 368, 370
  New Jersey, 388
  Oregon, 439

Quattlebaum, Charles A., 530
Quindry, Kenneth E., 730
Quinn, Pamela P., 443

Rand Corporation, 162, 192, 601-07
Ranney, Victoria, 290
Rapp, M. L., 602
Raymond, George M., 413
Reagan, Ronald, 261
  See also California-Governor
Reed, Wayne O., 492
Reese, Bonnie, 472
Reinhold, Robert, 36
Resnick, Michael A., 37
Reutter, E. Edmund, Jr., 117
Revenue sharing, 534
Reynolds, Jerry D., 609
Ribich, Thomas I., 663
Ridenour, Patricia, 316
Ridenour, Philip, 316
Riew, John, 207
Riles, Wilson, 528, 634
Ripon Society of Nashville, 668
Rochester Center for Governmental and Community Research, Inc., 414
Rolph, Earl R., 748
Rosenthal, Jack, 610
Rossmiller, Richard A., 469
Rowland, Howard S., 493

Rural population, 172
Ryan, Charlotte, 332
Ryan, Leo, 634, 669

Sabulao, Cesar M., 79
St. Louis, Mo. Public Schools, 373
San Francisco, Calif. Board of Education, 670
Sanchez, David, 634
Saretsky, Gary, 611
Saunders, Charles B., Jr., 116, 534
Schiller, Jeffry, 612
Schilling, Richard C., 490
Schoettle, Ferdinand P., 87
Schwartz, Ronald, 613, 614
Seitz, Reynolds C., 118
Selden, David, 640
Semple, Robert B., Jr., 731
Sensenbaugh, James A., 329
Sgontz, L. G., 729
Shaffer, Helen B., 164
Shanks, Hershel, 88
Shannon, John, 91, 152, 208, 325
Shannon, Thomas A., 269
Shoup, Carl S., 732
Silard, John, 23, 89, 90
Silk, Leonard, 733-35
Simat, Heilleisen and Eichner, Inc., 106
Simonetti, Gilbert J., 736
Sizer, Theodore R., 671
Sklar, Sigmund L., 105, 109
Smith, Dan T., 680, 737, 748
Smith, George C., 149
Smith, Mark C., 412
Soule, Don M., 320, 321
South Carolina. General Assembly. Committee to Study... Revenue for Educational Purposes, 448
South Dakota
  Legislative Research Council, 449-52
  School financing, 449-52
Southern Center for Studies in Public Policy, 495
Spaght, Samuel, 546
Stafford, F. F., 444

Stam, Jerome M., 167
Star, Jack, 615
State funding of education,
101, 124, 130, 141, 151,
173-472
Steinhilber, August W., 163
Stephenson, Jack G., 323
Stephenson, Richard C., 323
Stiles, Lynn A., 497
Stone Soup, 548
Stronberg, Joel B., 424, 425
Stuart, Patricia, 279
Stucker, James P., 192, 604-07
Sugarman, Stephan, 23, 636
Sullivan, Clara K., 738
Sullivan, Neil, 634
Sumner, G. C., 602
Surrey, Stanley S., 739, 751
Swenson, Norman P., 537
Syracuse University Research
Corporation, 496

Talley, Wayne K., 321
Tax Foundation, 165, 740
Tax Institute of America, 497,
741, 742
Tax Reform Research Group, 61
Tax Research Conference, Sioux
City, 311
Taxation With Representation,
743
Temple University, 440
Tennessee-School financing,
375
Texarkana, Ark.-School con-
tract, 192, 541, 549, 564,
567, 598, 602, 621
Texas
Committee on State and Lo-
cal Tax Policy, 453
Governor's Committee on Pub-
lic School Education, 454,
455
Legislative Council, 456
School financing, 47, 51,
55, 56, 64, 453-58
University. Institute of
Public Affairs, 457
Texas Research League, 458
Thackrey, Russell I., 673

Thatcher, George W., 426
Thomas, J. Alan, 190, 209,
345, 441
Tiedt, Sidney W., 498
Toledo Area Governmental Re-
search Association, 427-31
Twin Cities Area-Tax policy,
360, 362, 363

Ukockis, James R., 223
Ulmer, Melville J., 746
United States
Advisory Commission on In-
tergovernmental Rela-
tions, 41, 62, 91, 113,
166, 173, 190, 210-20,
682, 684-86
Congress. House, 499-501,
747
Committee on Education
and Labor, 502-09, 628
Committee on Ways and
Means, 748
Republican Task Force on
Education, 510
Congress. Joint Economic
Committee, 749-51
Congress. Senate, 511-13,
616, 752
Committee on Government
Operations, 514, 515
Committee on Labor and
Public Welfare, 485,
516-22
Republican Policy Commit-
tee, 221
Select Committee on Equal
Educational Opportunity,
523
Constitution, 73, 78, 80,
84, 310
Department of Agriculture,
167
Department of Health, Edu-
cation and Welfare, 199,
222, 602, 603
Ad Hoc Group on School
Finance, 524
Secretary, 527
Urban Education Task Force,
528

United States
Department of the Treasury,
529, 744, 754
District Court
Minnesota. Third Division,
63
Texas. San Antonio Divi-
sion, 64
Federal Reserve Bank
Boston, 92
Kansas City, 223
Philadelphia, 445-47, 674,
753
Library of Congress
Congressional Research
Service, 168
Legislative Reference
Service, 514, 530
Office of Economic Oppor-
tunity, 192, 560, 565,
594, 623, 660, 679
Office of Education, 93,
169, 334, 474, 507, 525,
526, 625
President, 531-35, 681-83
President's Commission on
School Finance, 100-14,
166, 220
Upper Midwest Research and De-
velopment Council, 370
Urban Coalition, 94, 356
Urban Institute, 95-97, 110,
271
Utah. Legislative Council, 459

Value-added tax, 149, 160,
680-756
Virginia
Commission to Study...State
Aid to Public Schools,
461
Division of State Planning
and Community Affairs,
462
School financing, 46, 460-
62
Vouchers, 101, 112, 152, 192,
194, 622-79

Walker, Mabel, 65, 97, 170
Wanniski, Jude, 745

Wardle, F., 677
Washington
Legislature
Joint Committee on Educa-
tion, 463-65
Legislative Budget Commit-
tee, 466
Special Levy Study Commis-
sion, 467
School financing, 463-68
Superintendent of Public
Instruction, 468
Washington University. Insti-
tute for Urban and Regional
Studies, 374, 375, 536
Watson, Philip E., 29
Watson Initiative, 241
Webb, Harold, 29, 171
Wegryn, James, 352
Weidenbaum, Murray L., 537
Weil, Roman L., 626
Weiss, Steven J., 92
West, E. G., 678
Westchester County, N.Y.
Department of Planning, 415
Western Kentucky University,
318
Westmeyer, Troy R., 66
Westmeyer, Wesley, 66
White, Sharon, 90
Whitman, Ray D., 328
Whitten, Phillip, 671
Wichita, Kan.-Performance
contracting, 546
Wicklander, Edgar B., 272
Willingham, Ed, 538, 620,
679
Wilson, Alan B., 93
Wilson, John, 583, 621
Wing, Richard L., 493
Wisconsin
Governor's Commission on
Education, 471
Legislative Council, 67
School financing, 469-72
Task Force on Local Govern-
ment Finance..., 472
University. Department of
Educational Administra-
tion, 159
Voucher plan, 673

Wise, Arthur E., 43, 44, 70,
  99, 104, 163
Woodard, Francis O.
  135
Woollatt, Lorne H.,
  497
Wynne, Edward, 134

Young Democratic Clubs of
  Maryland, 330
Yudof, Mark G., 43

Zazzera, Edmund, 192
Zimmer, John M., 172
Zukosky, Jerome, 45